Understanding God's Call:
A Ministry Inquiry Process

The United Methodist Church
2009 Edition

Richard Hunt
Sondra Matthaei
Sharon Rubey

Understanding God's Call: A Ministry Inquiry Process is designed to be completed with a guide. Contact your district superintendent or pastor and ask to be assigned a guide who will assist you in this study.

Copyright © 1997 (updated 2009) by the General Board of Higher Education and Ministry, The United Methodist Church, Nashville, Tennessee. All rights reserved.

United Methodist churches and other official United Methodist bodies may reproduce up to 1,000 words from this publication, provided the following notice appears with the excerpted material: "From *Understanding God's Call: A Ministry Inquiry Process.* Copyright © 1997 (updated 2009) by the General Board of Higher Education and Ministry, The United Methodist Church. Used by permission." Requests for quotations that exceed 1,000 words should be addressed to the Office of Interpretation, General Board of Higher Education and Ministry, PO Box 340007, Nashville, TN 37203-0007.

Unless otherwise noted, Scripture quotations are from the New Revised Standard Version Bible. Copyright © 1989 by the Division of Christian Education of the National Council of the Churches of Christ in the USA. Used by permission.

Disciplinary quotations are from *The Book of Discipline of The United Methodist Church – 2008.* Copyright © 2008 by The United Methodist Publishing House. Used by permission.

Quotations are taken from *The United Methodist Book of Worship.* Copyright © 1992 by The United Methodist Publishing House. Used by permission.

Printed in the United States of America.

ISBN 978-0-938162-82-7

Cover design by Laura L. Deck

Photography credits: Vicki Brown/General Board of Higher Education and Ministry, page 2; Mike DuBose/United Methodist Communications, page 22; Vicki Brown/ General Board of Higher Education and Ministry, page 44; Mike DuBose/United Methodist Communications, page 62; Perkins School of Theology, page 104; Mike DuBose/United Methodist Communications, page 126; Jack Corn, page 142; Saint Paul School of Theology, page 158.

Additional copies of *Understanding God's Call: A Ministry Inquiry Process* are available for $10.95 each from Cokesbury at 1-800-672-1798 or at www.cokesbury.com.

Contents

Acknowledgments iv

An Introduction for the Reader v

Basic Information Form vi

Candidacy Process vii

Session 1: Sharing Your Faith Story 1

Session 2: The Bible And God's Call 21

Session 3: Practicing God's Presence 43

Session 4: Your Heritage And Influences–Common And Unique 61

Session 5: Hearing God's Call To Your Future 85

Session 6: Living Your Spiritual Heritage 103

Session 7: Your United Methodist Heritage 125

Session 8: What Gift Can I Bring? 141

Session 9: Ministry Options To Explore 157

Annotated Bibliography 183

Appendices
    A. Models for Spiritual Discernment 190

    B. Group Model 194

    C. Denominational Resources for Further Growth 196

Acknowledgments

Revision Committee:

Beth Downs
John Edd Harper
Richard Hunt
Robert Kohler
Sondra Matthaei
Clara Reed
Carole Rooks
Sharon Rubey
Cean Wilson

"What Are You Doing?"

An Introduction For The Reader

"What are you doing?" the three workers were asked.
"I'm laying stones," said the first.
"I'm building a building," replied the second.
"I'm raising a cathedral for the worship of God!" exclaimed the third.

"What are you doing?" the teachers were asked.
"I'm putting up with these kids," said the first.
"I'm teaching these children to share," replied the second.
"I'm showing these future leaders how to live for God!" exclaimed the third.

What are you doing? is your lifelong question. Whatever your job, work, career, or vocation, what difference are you making in the world? How is your faith expressed through your work? Is your work a calling from God? In what ways are you in ministry?

Understanding God's Call: A Ministry Inquiry Process enables you to consider how God calls you through your interests and skills, through the world's needs, and throughout your life. Join in exploring how your life career path can become a vocation—making vocal God's calling to loving service.

A Ministry Inquiry Process is designed for any Christian to explore how faith and vocation are related. The issues and dimensions of one's faith journey, Bible, heritage, and future challenge every person, at any age, and in any vocation. In this exciting depth study you can renew and expand your own vision of how your gifts and fruit can express God's grace to you now.

If you are searching for God's will in your life, you are a seeker. If you have been trained to share your learning and experience to accompany another person on a faith journey, you are a guide. This exploration invites you to join together in a shared journey with God's Spirit.

Basic Information About Seekers

The seeker is invited to complete this get acquainted form to share with the guide at the time of their first meeting.

Personal information

Seeker's name _____age _____

Address _____

_____

Telephone: (home) _____

(office) _____ (school) _____

Fax _____ E-Mail: _____

Your local church _____

City _____
Briefly describe involvement in your local church, such as leadership positions you have held, groups you enjoy, etc., and involvement in activities beyond your local church such as church meetings, summer camp, etc.

_____

_____

_____

Denominational background

If you have participated as a member of other denominations, name them.

_____

_____

Educational background

High school _____

College _____

Other _____

Candidacy Process for the Deacon, Elder, and Local Pastor

Inquiring Candidate: *2008 Book of Discipline* ¶311

1. Contact your pastor, district superintendent (DS), or another deacon or elder
2. Read *The Christian as Minister* (recommended, not required)
3. Participate in *A Ministry Inquiry Process* (recommended, not required)

Beginning Candidacy: ¶311.1.a–c

1. Member of The United Methodist Church or baptized participant of a recognized United Methodist campus ministry or other United Methodist ministry setting for one (1) year
2. Apply to DS in writing, including statement of call; ask for admission to candidacy program and assignment of a candidacy mentor
3. Complete candidacy online enrollment and $75 payment
4. Complete beginning stages of candidacy with candidacy mentor

Declaring Candidacy: ¶311.1.d, e

1. High school degree or equivalent is required
2. Request interview by Pastor/Staff Parish Relations Committee or equivalent in your ministry setting; provide statement of call; and responses to disciplinary questions in ¶310
3. Request recommendation by charge conference or equivalent as specified by district committee
4. Continue candidacy program with candidacy mentor and academic requirements

Certified Candidacy: ¶311.2

Completion of the following:
1. Written response to ministry questions in ¶311.2a as well as ¶310
2. Psychological assessment, criminal background, and credit check
3. Notarized statement certifying have neither been accused in writing nor convicted of a felony, misdemeanor, or any incident of sexual misconduct or child abuse
4. Provide other information upon request
5. Agree to make a complete dedication to the highest ideals of the Christian life
6. Examination and approval by district committee on ordained ministry

Local Pastor - Completed candidacy certification, licensed, and assigned a clergy mentor ¶314

Continuing Candidacy: ¶312

1. Annual recommendation by charge conference
2. Annual interview and approval by district committee
3. Annual report of satisfactory progress of studies and copy of transcripts from university or school of theology

Completing Candidacy: ¶324

1. Certified candidate for minimum of one (1) year, maximum twelve (12) years
2. One (1) year in service ministry
3. Completion of one-half the basic graduate theological studies to be eligible for commissioning
4. Health certificate completed by medical doctor
5. Written and oral doctrinal exam and written autobiographical statement
6. Interview and recommendation by three-fourths vote of district committee
7. Interview and recommendation by the board or ordained ministry
8. Election to provisional membership by clergy session

Commissioned to ministry of elder or deacon as provisional member

41436-08/04

Session 1

Sharing Your Faith Story

Ask, and it will be given to you; search, and you will find; knock, and the door will be opened for you.

(Matthew 7:7)

Centering Moments

Philip and the Ethiopian Eunuch

Then an angel of the Lord said to Philip, "Get up and go toward the south to the road that goes down from Jerusalem to Gaza," So he got up and went. Now there was an Ethiopian eunuch, a court official of the Candace, queen of the Ethiopians, in charge of her entire treasury. He had come to Jerusalem to worship and was returning home; seated in his chariot, he was reading the prophet Isaiah. Then the Spirit said to Philip, "Go over to this chariot and join it." So Philip ran up to it and heard him reading the prophet Isaiah. He asked, "Do you understand what you are reading?" He replied, "How can I, unless someone guides me?" And he invited Philip to get in and sit beside him. . . .

Then Philip began to speak, and starting with this scripture, he proclaimed to him the good news about Jesus. As they were going along the road, they came to some water; and the eunuch said, "Look, here is water! What is to prevent me from being baptized?" He commanded the chariot to stop, and both of them, Philip and the eunuch, went down into the water, and Philip baptized him.

Acts 8:26-31; 35-38

The Conversion of Lydia

(Paul and Timothy) set sail from Troas and took a straight course to Samothrace, the following day to Neapolis, and from there to Philippi, which is a leading city of the district of Macedonia and a Roman colony. We remained in this city for some days. On the Sabbath day we went outside the gate by the river, where we supposed there was a place of prayer; and we sat down and spoke to the women who had gathered there. A certain woman named Lydia, a worshiper of God, was listening to us; she was from the city of Thyatira and a dealer in purple cloth. The Lord opened her heart to listen eagerly to what was said by Paul. When she and her household were baptized, she urged us, saying, "If you have judged me to be faithful to the Lord, come and stay at my home." And she prevailed upon us.

Acts 16:11-15

Purpose of this session:

This session provides an opportunity for the seeker and guide to get acquainted, to review Understanding God's Call: A Ministry Inquiry Process, *to plan future sessions, and to make a mutual commitment to share this spiritual journey together.*

Introduction

The central question in *A Ministry Inquiry Process* is: *What is God calling me to do at this time and how shall I respond?*

Put another way, *how may I understand God's calling to me at this time, and how will I change in response?*

This process is intended to assist any person in The United Methodist Church to listen anew to God's call and to respond accordingly.

Establishing Your Relationship

Notes:

Begin this session by sharing basic biographical information with each other; then turn to your life journeys and spiritual turning points. Select one or more of the following to discuss:

1. Read the account of Jeremiah's call in Jeremiah 1:4-10 and talk about how your spiritual journey is similar to or different from Jeremiah's experience.

Both the seeker and the guide come to this relationship with unique gifts and graces to share. It is important to begin building a relationship of mutual trust while recognizing that there is a difference in positions in the relationship.

2. Share reflections on these questions:

   a. What does it mean to live a Christian life?

Your relationship is intended to be one of mutual sharing. Both the seeker and the guide need to be open to each other. Both will be changed by A Ministry Inquiry Process.

   b. What images of God have influenced or emerged from your journeys?

Notes:

It would be appropriate for developing a mutual relationship for the guide to share answers to these questions as well.

c. How has your relation with God developed and changed over time?

d. What are your dreams for the future?

3. Share what you bring to the process at this particular time, including previous study and experience with readings, conferences, significant relationships, etc.

a. What are you excited about?

b. What questions/concerns do you have?

The *Ministry Inquiry Process*

Notes:

This process offers opportunities for spiritual discernment in which **both** seeker and guide endeavor to follow God's leading in this shared spiritual journey.

The Role of the Seeker

The focus is a free and open exploration of the seeker's own sense of God's calling.

At this point, you may have experienced an undefined drawing, pull, or attraction to explore ministry options, but may not yet see these experiences as "call."

What is most important is that you explore your relationship with God knowing that the church supports you as you consider the direction of your life by providing a guide who will lead you in your exploration.

In this exploration, you are seeking to know God's call more clearly so you can respond. As the seeker, your spiritual journey is the focus of the *Ministry Inquiry Process*, and your guide serves as a mentor, guide, and friend.

The only qualification as a seeker is the desire to examine your life situation in relation to God's call to serve the needs of the world as God's creation.

What does seeker mean to you? What other terms describe your role in the *Ministry Inquiry Process*?

Some seekers may not be clear about their vocational identity and/or call and may be just beginning to explore the claim of God on their lives. An additional resource about discerning God's call is Yearning to Know God's Will *by Danny Morris.*

Other seekers may not have much experience in spiritual formation and discernment. Appendix A on page 190 in this guidebook offers models for spiritual discernment.

Discuss these questions together.

The Role of the Guide

The guide in this process can be any committed Christian—lay, diaconal, deacon in full connection, or elder—who has already experienced God's call and responded by seeking guidance and discernment in her or his own life through this or other similar programs.

Your guide is making his or her wisdom, expertise, and spiritual discernment available for your growth.

What does the word "guide" mean to you? What other terms describe the help you want from your guide in this process?

Self-awareness on the part of the guide will support the seeker's spiritual journey.

Discuss these questions together.

Notes:

The role of the guide is to affirm the journey without saying no to any direction the seeker may consider. Yet the guide needs to be able to raise issues and questions for growth.

Your guide has been selected by the church because she or he gives evidence of spiritual maturity, knows about the spiritual dimensions of the vocational process, and is familiar with the roles of lay person, diaconal minister, deacon in full connection, and elder in The United Methodist Church.

The process is confidential. Your guide does not report to any board, committee, or agency, or share details of your sessions.

Ministry

In this process "to minister" means to serve God in any way—as part of the ministry of all Christians, or as part of ordained ministry as deacon in full connection or elder.

The term "ministry" may be a bit confusing because it once referred to the pastor or staff of a local church. Here ministry includes all types of work that Christians do in the world.

What does the word "ministry" mean to you? Give some examples.

You will explore the meaning of ministry in more depth as you move through the process.

An Overview of the *Ministry Inquiry Process*

Notes:

Goals

The overall goal of the *Ministry Inquiry Process* is that you, as a seeker, will be strengthened in your spiritual life and encouraged in your service as you follow God's leading.

The intent of this process is to enable you, working with your guide, to

1. **come to know God's call and to recognize the gifts you bring to ministry;**

2. **learn more about ways you might respond to God's love through ministry and service;**

3. **establish a plan to obtain more information about ministry options and move toward definite decisions concerning how your sense of call fits with the ministry and mission of The United Methodist Church.**

According to your discoveries you will then be able to identify more specific goals and select one or more subsequent paths to explore further. These may include a variety of career areas in which lay Christians work, as well as candidacy for ordained ministry as deacon in full connection or elder.

Do the goals of the process fit the personal goals you have brought to this process? Talk with your guide about how you feel about them so far.

Vision

The primary **vision** is that the *Ministry Inquiry Process* will be the initial step for you as seeker to

1. **discuss your calling and vocational directions with a guide;**

2. **understand the ministry of all Christians and ordained ministries of deacon in full connection and elder in The United Methodist Church, and then decide whether to explore one or more in greater depth.**

You may choose some of these ways to explore the overview of the Ministry Inquiry Process*:*

1. As you talk about the goals of the Ministry Inquiry Process, *discuss the following questions.*
   a. How do you cultivate your awareness of God at work in your lives (discernment)?
   b. What other ways of finding God's direction for your lives would you like to explore?

2. For resources about spiritual discernment, refer to Session 3, "Practicing God's Presence" (page 43), and Appendix A (page 190) in this guidebook.

3. You will also want to share expectations for this Ministry Inquiry Process.

Notes:

a. *What does the seeker expect and what does the guide expect?*

b. *What is your expected outcome for the process itself?*

What questions do you have about the goals and vision of the process ?

Outcome

When the *Ministry Inquiry Process* is completed, an outcome report will be prepared by you and your guide. With your permission, your guide will keep a copy of this report.

If you need the *Ministry Inquiry Process* certification to continue into an exploration track for candidacy for ordained ministry as deacon in full connection or elder, your guide will certify that you have completed this this introductory process to the candidacy registrar of the Conference Board of Ordained Ministry.

You are responsible for keeping this outcome report for use in a candidacy track if you choose one.

The Design

The design of the *Ministry Inquiry Process* includes nine (9) sessions. Each session is planned for two hours with meetings approximately two to six weeks apart.

Sessions
1. **Sharing Your Faith Story**
2. **The Bible and God's Call**
3. **Practicing God's Presence**
4. **Your Heritage and Influences—Common and Unique**
5. **Hearing God's Call To Your Future**
6. **Living Your Spiritual Heritage**
7. **Your United Methodist Heritage**
8. **What Gift Can I Bring?**
9. **Ministry Options To Explore**

Look through the sessions together now. What do you see that connects with your spiritual journey? What sessions look particularly helpful to you? What sessions contain material that is familiar to you? New to you? Use these questions to help you and your guide determine how much time to spend on each session.

Optional Group Retreat Sessions

Appendix B on page 196 in this guidebook contains a group model for use in a retreat setting for one guide and a small group of seekers.

About this Guidebook

This guidebook provides prayers, information, questions, space to make notes and comments, and resources to aid your journey of vocational discernment. The open format encourages both seeker and guide to read all pages and modify them to fit the needs of both persons.

Although the main part of this guidebook is addressed to the seeker, the guide will also be reviewing it again. Notes on the side of the page address the guide as consultant, but they are also intended for review by the seeker. In this way, both persons can continue in a mutual covenant of spiritual exploration and discernment.

Each session is oriented toward helping you more clearly define your relationship with God. The time with your guide will focus on your spiritual journey—your relationship with God, and your response to God's love in your life.

Covenant together to conduct each session in an attitude of prayer through thoughtful listening and speaking to each other and to God, and pray for each other during this process.

Ways to use this guidebook for both seeker and guide:

- Read through the material for your session before meeting together.
- Decide what to prepare in advance.
- Note questions that arise during your preparation and bring them for discussion.
- Bring your own spiritual resources to share.

Supplementary Resources for Sessions

In addition to the Bible and this guidebook, four basic United Methodist resources will be helpful for your spiritual journey regardless of the direction you take. These are:

The Book of Discipline of The United Methodist Church
The Christian As Minister
The United Methodist Hymnal—1989
The United Methodist Book of Worship—1992

The United Methodist Hymnal and *The United Methodist Book of Worship* can be especially useful for individual and family worship as well as congregational worship. These two resources provide a wide variety of hymns and prayers that you may use in your sessions with your guide.

Both of these resources have lists of references that are helpful. For example, page 497 of *The United Methodist Book of Worship* has a list of prayers that are contained in *The United Methodist Hymnal*. Note also the listing of hymns and prayers in the "Index of Topics and Categories" in the back of *The United Methodist Hymnal*.

You will be using the *Book of Discipline* to study what it means to be United Methodist, as well as the requirements for the ministry of all Christians and ordained ministry as deacon in full connection or elder.

You need to have regular access to these resources as part of this process. You may purchase them from Cokesbury (1-800-672-1789 or www.cokesbury.com) for your own personal use and notation.

Reflection

This part of each session is time for reflection. Be open to the Holy Spirit's leading. Enter any notes in the space provided to aid you in this process.

Our Mutual Commitment

Notes:

Your mutual commitment will provide guidance for the *Ministry Inquiry Process*. You and your guide need to agree on the kind of relationship that will be most helpful for the work you will do.

Talk about the things that are most important to you in a trusting relationship.

Part of your agreement is that you will work through each session together. As seeker, you may stop the process at the end of any session, but you are asked not to drop out mid session without mutual agreement.

What do you expect of each other?

On the following pages, record the plan for the rest of your time together as a reminder of your mutual commitment in light of your relationship to God.

Notes:

When you outline your study plan, decide how much time should be devoted to each session.

Allow time for reflection and breaks, noted in each session as "Reflection."

Develop the mutual commitment as a draft in the first session; then address it at the beginning of the second session to see if anything needs to be changed after you have had time to reflect on it.

Our Plan

1. Examine the sessions. Plan assignments and learning experiences using the sessions listed on page 10.

UNDERSTANDING GOD'S CALL: A MINISTRY INQUIRY PROCESS   15

2. Schedule meeting dates two to six weeks apart. Discuss how you might
   negotiate a more detailed time line if that would be helpful in completing
   assignments. Record your meeting dates and time line here:

Session number   Date   Place

_____

_____

_____

_____

_____

_____

_____

_____

3. Exchange telephone numbers in case you need to contact each other to
   share information or adjust meeting times.

_____

_____

4. Define responsibilities. In preparing for sessions, or in work and reflection
   between sessions, what will the guide do? What will the seeker do?

5. How will you record your progress? Will you write insights and questions in this guidebook as you go?

Other options for recording your insights and growth include an audio-tape or handwritten journal, a collage of images, a musical reflection, a computer word processing file.

6. What spiritual practices will you use to keep the focus of these sessions on God at work in your lives? Options include fasting, meditation, journaling, Scripture study, spiritual direction, various kinds of worship, singing, liturgical movement, regular participation in Holy Communion.

Note here the spiritual practices that are helpful for you.

7. Allow time at the end of the session to identify and plan for your next steps. Review the notes for your next session to see what advance preparation may be required.

Review and Closing

Notes:

Review what has happened in this session and where you now are concerning your sense of call and vocational decision process.

This point in the session is a helpful time to evaluate how the Ministry Inquiry Process is developing.

What observations and recommendations does your guide have from your time together?

If, at any point, the seeker decides not to continue, assist the seeker to find alternatives for spiritual and vocational growth. Lead a prayer of affirmation and sending forth.

Review the notes for the next session and decide what to prepare in advance.

From the list of resources on pages 18-19, select a hymn and/or prayer to use in celebration of the time you have shared. One possibility is the "Sarum Blessing," *The United Methodist Book of Worship,* #566.

If the seeker is continuing the Ministry Inquiry Process with you, affirm your covenant in the closing worship moments.

Resources

Needed during session

Bible
The United Methodist Hymnal
The United Methodist Book of Worship

Recommended books

Millard, Kent. *Get Acquainted with Your Christian Faith*. Leader's Guide and Study Book. Nashville: Abingdon Press, 1996.

Morris, Danny. *Yearning to Know God's Will: A Workbook for Discerning God's Guidance for Your Life*. Grand Rapids, Mich.: Zondervan Publishing House, 1991.

Hymns

From *The United Methodist Hymnal*
"Tell Me the Stories of Jesus," #277
"Jesus Calls Us," #398
"Take My Life, and Let It Be," #399
"The Voice of God is Calling," #436
"What Does the Lord Require?" #441
"We've a Story to Tell to the Nations," #569
"Go, Make of All Disciples," #571
"Pass It On," #572
"Sois la Semilla (You Are the Seed)," #583
"Many Gifts, One Spirit," #114
"What Gift Can We Bring?" #87
"I Love to Tell the Story," #156
"Lord, I Want to Be A Christian," #402

Prayers

From *The United Methodist Hymnal*
"O Love That Wilt Not Let Me Go," #480
"For God's Gifts," #489
"For Holiness of Heart," #401
"Prayer of Ignatius of Loyola," #570

From *The United Methodist Book of Worship*
"Offertory Hymn: For the Gift of Creation," #179
"Call to Prayer," #196
"For Discernment, #510
"For Guidance," #512
"For the Mind of Christ," #514
"For Wisdom," #525
"Prayers of Thanksgiving After the Offering," #550
"Daily Praise and Prayer" #568-580

Session 2

The Bible and God's Call

He went up to the mountain and called to him those whom he wanted, and they came to him.

(Mark 3:13)

Centering Moments

Jesus Calls the First Disciples

As Jesus passed along the Sea of Galilee, he saw Simon and his brother Andrew casting a net into the sea—for they were fishermen. And Jesus said to them, "Follow me and I will make you fish for people." And immediately they left their nets and followed him. As he went a little farther, he saw James son of Zebedee and his brother John, who were in their boat mending the nets. Immediately he called them; and they left their father Zebedee in the boat with the hired men and followed him.

Mark 1:16-20

Purpose of this session:

The purpose of this session is for you to explore the Bible and God's call in some depth by thinking about the different ways God calls persons, including you, to faith and service.

Introduction

God calls persons in a variety of ways. In this session you will focus specifically on examples of God's calling in the Bible in an attempt to discern how God is calling you.

Spiritual discernment means paying attention to God's call in your life and coming to know God's direction for your life.

In Scripture, God's calling comes through healing, teaching, and sending, the heart of the "good news" of God's grace and responses in faith to this gospel.

This process will help you clarify your call, name obstacles or areas where healing is needed, identify gifts and graces to be nurtured, and define a particular response to God's calling.

Calling Through Healing, Teaching, and Sending

Calling

"Calling" is when someone gets your attention and engages you in a relationship. The name you call someone else establishes a relationship that identifies both you and the other person. To call "Hey, you!" is different from calling you by either an affectionate or a derogatory name.

Your parents or significant caregivers called you by name when you were a young child. Later you chose either to accept that name or change it in some way, perhaps using different nicknames according to the different groups in which you were involved.

Calling comes out of a relationship with God. In Scripture, calling is when God initially reaches out to a person or group. Sometimes God calls in very dramatic and unexpected ways, and at other times God calls in quiet, routine, or predictable experiences.

The Gospels describe how Jesus called the twelve disciples or apostles to go and serve (Mark 3:13-19, Matthew 10:1-4, Luke 6:12-16). There are many other instances when Jesus invited his followers to come to him. At other times, there was an implied calling when Jesus' fame drew crowds to him for healing and teaching.

God's Call in the Bible

1. With your guide, read and discuss one or more of these biblical examples of calling:

Old Testament
- Jacob, Genesis 32:22-32
- Esther, Esther 4
- Isaiah, Isaiah 6
- Jeremiah, Jeremiah 1:4-19
- Ezekiel, Ezekiel 1-3

Notes:

Calling through healing, teaching, and sending may happen simultaneously—all are a gift of God's grace.

Some suggestions about how to address this section on God's calling include:

1. The theme of God's calling through healing, teaching, and sending appears in each of the four Gospels. You may want to read rapidly through one of the four Gospels without pausing for details to see how God calls persons in a variety of ways.

2. Examine the calling of the disciples. Look for examples of how God calls through healing, teaching, and sending.

3. You may want to find a place in the Gospel of Mark where Jesus is described as calling a person or group. Then move to an account of healing, teaching, or sending to find another example of God's calling.

Notes:

New Testament
- Zechariah and Elizabeth, Luke 1
- Mary, Luke 1
- John the Baptist, Luke 3:1-20
- Timothy, 2 Timothy 3:10-4:5
- Disciples, Mark 3:13-19, Matthew 10:1-4, Luke 6: 12-16

4. As an alternate approach, use a concordance to find one or two accounts of God's calling in the Old and/or New Testament that are especially meaningful to you. Bring your notes to the session for discussion.

a. How does God's call come to the persons involved?

b. How does each person respond? To what extent is each person confident, hesitant, willing, or uncertain? How does each person feel about her/his call?

c. In your New Testament example, talk about the ways God in Christ offers healing and reassurance to the person called.

d. To what task is each called? How do these tasks differ among the persons called at different times?

Notes:

As a guide, be prepared to share your own call or calls with the seeker.

God's Call in Your Life

1. What are some other examples of God's callings that you have experienced or heard about?

2. God's call to you is your special invitation to respond. Calling happens when you feel drawn, attracted, compelled, fascinated, or curious about something. Something or someone has your attention. The next task is to discover who has called you and why.

   You have answered God's invitation by participating in the *Ministry Inquiry Process*. Now your task is to clarify the call and determine your response.

a. In what ways did God call you?

    a. Describe some ways you are aware of God's calling you.

b. How did you know God was calling you?

    b. What insights and discoveries from your study of biblical call help you understand your own experience?

God's Call through the Sacraments

Notes:

God calls you through the sacraments of Baptism and the Lord's Supper. These serve as reminders of God's grace in the very basic human experiences of birth, naming, meals, and other experiences of physical and spiritual nurture in your family or in other close relationships—both growing up and currently.

1. Tell the story of your baptism. How does God call you through your baptism?

   As a guide, be prepared to share your own story of baptism.

2. Recall a memorable time at the Lord's Table. How does God call you through Communion?

   As a guide, be prepared to share your own experience of the Lord's Supper.

Reflection

- Do I desire to hear and do God's will?

- Do I want to live a life aligned with God's will for me, regardless of where that commitment will take me?

- Am I going to trust God with my future?

These questions are for personal reflection at this point. They could be the focus of a time of silent meditation.

Notes:

God's calling may come through the healing power of God's grace, but healing may also be a response to God's calling.

What terms or metaphors would you use for healing?

Name all the different ways the word "healing" might be used.

Healing

The Holy Spirit helps you hear God's call through healing. Healing may be needed to overcome obstacles that keep you from responding to God's calling. Healing gives you the eyes and ears of faith so you can understand God's teachings, receive the nurture of the Holy Spirit, and respond to God's call.

There are many terms or metaphors for your spiritual being that God heals such as will, heart, motivation, attitude, mind, depths of being, and right relationship. All of these are helpful, yet none of the terms fully describes the awe and mystery of the Holy Spirit's indwelling and healing.

What does the word "healing" mean to you?

Calling and Healing in the Bible

Jesus said that he has come to heal those who are sick or bound by sin (*see Luke 5:31-32*). When you are healed by God through the Holy Spirit, your relationship with God is restored. You are aware that God loves you, is continually seeking to be reconciled with you, and is calling you to go and serve.

Consider the hymn "When Jesus the Healer Passed Through Galilee" (*The United Methodist Hymnal*, #263).

1. Note the many instances of Jesus' healing others.

2. How did the persons respond to the healing?

Notes:

Calling and Healing in Your Life

Because Christians value physical healing in all its forms, physical healing serves as a metaphor pointing to the work of the Holy Spirit in changing heart or attitude, bringing wholeness. Healing helps you to be open to God's calling through teaching and nurture and then to go out in Christ's name to serve others.

As a guide, be prepared to share your experience of God's healing grace in your life.

1. Describe some of the ways you have experienced God's healing grace in your life.

2. How does the Holy Spirit open you to discerning God's call in your own life journey?

Reflection

These questions are for personal reflection at this point. They could be the focus of a time of silent meditation.

- What must I lay down and what must I take up in order to go forward with God without pre-judgment about what the direction will be or must be for me?

- What healing do I need in order to live in union of faith and love with God?

UNDERSTANDING GOD'S CALL: A MINISTRY INQUIRY PROCESS   33

Teaching

In the Gospels, accounts of Jesus' healing of one or more persons are usually followed with a parable, teaching, or interpretation. God calls persons to serve through teaching as preparation for being sent into the world.

Jesus' teaching in the Sermon on the Mount in Matthew 5-7 and Luke 6 assumes that people are able to see, hear, receive, and understand the Gospel. The Gospel calls people to live in God's way.

Notes:

Teaching is a response to God's calling, but God's calling also comes to persons through teaching.

If appropriate, you may want to extend your discussion of God's way by talking about kingdom or reign of God—God's larger vision for creation.

Calling and Teaching in the Bible

1. Read Matthew 5:1-12 and talk with your guide about what Jesus was trying to teach those who were present through the Beatitudes.

    a. What do the Beatitudes tell you about what it means to live in God's way (phrases beginning with "Blessed are . . .")?

    b. What is promised to those who live in God's way (phrases beginning with "for they . . .")?

c. How is God calling persons through Jesus' teaching in the Beatitudes?

d. How would you share the meaning of the Beatitudes in your own words?

2. List some of Jesus' teachings that are especially significant for you. What do they teach you about God's calling and living in God's way?

UNDERSTANDING GOD'S CALL: A MINISTRY INQUIRY PROCESS 35

Calling and Teaching in Your Life

Teaching and healing interact, nurturing both the receiver and the giver in many ways. God's healing restores persons to wholeness and brings reconciliation to relationships. Reconciliation helps both teacher and hearer see and hear by faith—to hear God's calling.

1. Think of one person whose life has affected you in important ways.

   a. In what ways has God's calling through healing and teaching been a part of this relationship?

   b. What have you learned from this person?

   c. How did this person nurture you and help give you a glimpse of God's reign?

Notes:

If it would be helpful, talk about how teaching and healing are related.

As a guide, think about an example from your own experience to share.

As guide, what examples of teaching and nurturing might you share?

2. Describe some of your own teaching and nurturing abilities. How have you taught or nurtured others? How might you participate in teaching others about God's way?

Reflection

These questions are for personal reflection at this point. They could be the focus of a time of silent meditation.

- What are the possible directions God is calling me and that I am prompted to take?

- What are my gifts and graces?

- What are the needs that touch me?

- What may be the best possible routes for me, given my gifts and graces?

Sending

Going out to serve in the world is a response to God's calling, but sending may also be a vehicle for God's call. In the going and serving, you may hear a further call.

Calling and Sending in the Bible

The Bible reports that Jesus calls disciples, and then through healing and teaching sends them out into the world (*see Luke 10, Luke 24*).

Read the Great Commission in Matthew 28:19-20. It clearly summarizes God's calling through healing, teaching, and sending disciples out into the world. What does it say to you?

An important meaning of every Christian's vocational journey is that God's calling through healing and teaching sends people out in God's service. A worship service ends by sending people into the world to serve as a healed and prepared (educated, trained) representative or disciple of Christ.

Calling and Sending in Your Life

Sending involves matching an inner call from God with an outward or external call from others for service. Discernment about how an external call to service fulfills your inner call from God will require careful assessment of your gifts and graces, listening to those who know you well, and praying for clarity to do God's will. In this process, you will work with your guide to form the best possible pictures or options for your response to God's call.

Answering the following questions may help you begin to clarify how God is calling you and where God is sending you. You may also revisit your own personal story and life journey to identify the talents and abilities God has given you.

This is only a beginning. You will have an opportunity later in the process to reflect on these areas, so note questions, as well as your first responses.

1. What are some needs of the world that challenge you?

2. What are some talents, gifts, skills, abilities that you have or could develop to meet these needs?

Notes:

3. Where do the needs of the world and your talents meet? How could you uniquely address the need?

Be prepared to share some examples of how your unique gifts intersect with the needs of the world.

4. Could you best minister to the need through a paid or volunteer position in a local church, a church agency, a parachurch or nonprofit organization, a government agency, a position in business or industry, or other paid or volunteer work?

Reflection

- As I set my preferences before God one at a time, with which do I have peace with God and sense God is sending me forward in faith?

- Which route opens the way for me to give fullest expression to my "Here am I" to the Lord and meets the human need toward which God has directed me?

These questions are for personal reflection at this point. They could be the focus of a time of silent meditation.

Review and Closing

Reflect on this session and be open to the Holy Spirit's leading.

1. What have you learned about God's calling through healing, teaching, and sending? Enter any notes to aid you in this process.

In the world you experience both victories and defeats. The din of other voices and forces can fatigue and temporarily overpower you. Therefore God's calling through healing, teaching, and sending begins every time God draws you back to Christ's body for healing and renewal. Daily and weekly calls to return to God's sanctuary for prayer and worship are an important way the Holy Spirit renews you for your good work in the world for God. Once renewed, the Spirit sends you out again to serve.

2. In what ways do you find renewal for your work in the world?

3. Review the notes for the next session and decide what to prepare in advance.

4. Select a hymn and a prayer from the resource list on page 41 as a way to close your session together.

Resources

Needed during session

Bible
The United Methodist Hymnal

Recommended books

Miller, Wendy. *Learning to Listen: A Guide for Spiritual Friends.* Nashville: Upper Room Books, 1993.

Parker, Simon. *The Call to Servant Leadership.* Nashville: Division of Diaconal Ministry, General Board of Higher Education and Ministry, The United Methodist Church, 1990.

Roth, Bob. *Answering God's Call for Your Life.* Nashville: Division of Ordained Ministry, General Board of Higher Education and Ministry, The United Methodist Church, 2006.

Hymns and prayers

From *The United Methodist Hymnal*
See the following categories in the Index of Topics and Categories, page 934.

"Call to the Christian Life"
"Healing"
"Education"
"Home and Family"
"Testimony and Witness"
"Sending Forth"

Session 3

Practicing God's Presence

Listen! I am standing at the door, knocking; if you hear my voice and open the door, I will come in to you and eat with you, and you with me.

(Revelation 3:20)

UNDERSTANDING GOD'S CALL: A MINISTRY INQUIRY PROCESS

Centering Moments

"Lord, Prepare Me To Be A Sanctuary"

Lord, prepare me to be a sanctuary,
Pure and holy, tried, and true,
And with thanksgiving I'll be a living
Sanctuary for you.

(Source unknown)

Notes:

If you prefer, you may focus your time together by sharing the act of "Daily Prayer and Praise" from The United Methodist Book of Worship, *568-578 and read the hymn "Lord, Prepare Me to Be A Sanctuary." Talk about what the words of the hymn mean to you.*

Notes:

Purpose of this session:

This session is directed to seekers who are not already using spiritual disciplines. It helps them expand their knowledge of these disciplines and initiate some practices to cultivate their spiritual lives.

A Holy Life

Before this session, read "The General Rules of the Methodist Church" in the Book of Discipline, ¶103.

As guide, be prepared to share what a holy life means to you.

How would you describe a holy life?

John Wesley, the founder of Methodism, knew that people need to cultivate their spiritual lives in community. The goal is for Christians to become more Christlike, or more holy, in their daily living. But it is not possible to do this alone. People need the company of other faithful Christians on their spiritual journeys.

1. Talk with your guide about what it means to become more Christlike. One common childhood prayer put it this way: "Help me to be more like Jesus every day."

2. List some ways you are seeking to make your life more holy through spiritual practices such as private prayer, public worship, Bible study, participating in Holy Communion, or serving others.

3. Talk with your guide about how these spiritual practices have raised questions about the meaning of faith for you.

4. What is it about these spiritual practices that is helpful for your growth in faith?

Means of Grace

Specific spiritual practices or disciplines helped early Methodists cultivate their spiritual lives. These practices were called the "means of grace."

John Wesley knew that God does not abandon people on their spiritual journeys. God provides the means of grace to help people leave their brokenness behind and continue on the way to wholeness through a deeper relationship with God. The means of grace are spiritual practices through which Christ may meet people of faith. These spiritual practices are a response to God who loved people first; they are not a way to earn God's love.

What spiritual practices have you used to cultivate your spiritual life and keep you focused on God? Which are most helpful to you in specific situations?

Acts of Piety

Spiritual disciplines established by Christ help Christians develop their relationship with God. These means of grace are called acts of piety:

1. *Prayer.* Prayer is essential to the Christian life because it opens the door to a richer relationship with God.

    a. What are some of the different ways that you pray?

    b. What are other methods of prayer that you might want to explore?

UNDERSTANDING GOD'S CALL: A MINISTRY INQUIRY PROCESS   49

2. ***Searching the Scriptures.*** God's love is revealed in Scripture. Through reading, hearing, and meditating on Scripture, Christians discover God's will and direction for them.

    a. Name some of your favorite verses, passages, or stories from Scripture and talk about why they are so important to you.

    b. What are some of the different ways you have studied Scripture? How has God been revealed to you through searching the Scriptures?

3. ***The Lord's Supper.*** Since Christ promised to meet people at the Lord's Supper, early Methodists were encouraged to participate in Holy Communion as often as possible.

    Talk about your participation in Holy Communion and what it means to your spiritual life.

4. ***Fasting.*** It is easy to lose focus on God through the distractions of the world. Fasting is one means of renewing an intention for a Christian life.

   a. Talk about your understanding and experience of fasting. What is its value as a spiritual practice?

   b. How might a person fast from something other than food, such as television or other distractions?

   c. Read ¶304.2 in the *Book of Discipline* and talk with your guide about the disciplined life required of persons in ministry.

5. **Christian Conference.** Nurture, support, and accountability are needed for faithful Christian discipleship. Gathering in small groups to share joys, burdens, and challenges in living Christlike lives was an important component of the early Methodist societies. United Methodists believe that conferencing is important for faithful Christian community.

Talk about how Christian conferencing contributes to the cultivation of your spiritual life.

Acts of Mercy

1. Wesley also believed that we meet God and God meets us through service. Acts of Christian service are ways of loving God and loving neighbor. These "acts of mercy" or practices of love are a way to build a life of Christian discipleship.

   a. In what ways have you served your neighbor through acts of mercy?

   b. How has your spiritual journey been affected by service to other persons? How have you served creation as a whole?

   c. What happens when you practice "random acts of kindness"?

UNDERSTANDING GOD'S CALL: A MINISTRY INQUIRY PROCESS   53

2. Review "Our Doctrinal Standards and General Rules of the Methodist Church" (*Book of Discipline*, ¶103) and select the rules that you do use or could use as spiritual disciplines for loving God and loving neighbor.

   a. doing no harm

   b. doing all the good you can

   c. attending upon the ordinances (worship and sacraments) of God

Reflection

Reflect on this session so far and be open to the Holy Spirit's leading. What have you learned about spiritual practices that could cultivate your spiritual life and keep you focused on God?

Notes:

If more experience in discernment is needed, use the resources in Appendix A, page 190, in this guidebook.

Spiritual Discernment

Living a spiritual life needs skills of spiritual discernment. Discernment means being able to tell the difference between God's voice and other voices. Brother Lawrence defined discernment as "practicing the presence of God."

Being aware of God's presence at work through the Holy Spirit in your everyday life requires practice. Discernment means learning to know what is of God and what is not.

1. Have there been some times in your life when you have been aware of the presence of God through the Holy Spirit? Talk with your guide about what it means to experience the presence of the Holy Spirit.

2. Discernment means having "eyes to see and ears to hear" God at work in people's lives and in the world.

   a. Are there times when you have seen God at work in the world?

   b. What was it that made you think you were seeing the work of the Holy Spirit?

3. Sometimes others may help you discern, discover, or appropriate the work of the Holy Spirit that you have not yet seen. Someone may say, "Do you know that you have a real gift for . . . " or "God was at work in that experience helping you."

   Can you think of times when other persons have discerned something about you which later helped you in your life of faith?

4. Spiritual discernment requires careful listening. By practicing silence and letting all of the busy thoughts go, you can open yourself to the work of the Holy Spirit. You become aware of God's presence by being silent.

   In the beginning, you may have to practice being silent for short periods of time because silence is often uncomfortable. You live in a world that expects you to be busy and productive.

   Practicing being silent allows you to withdraw from all distractions in order to focus intensively on God. It is active listening in the sense of responding to every incoming stimulus with the question, "Is this what God is saying to me or us?" Being silent is not so much imposed from without but rather being so focused on God that all other perceptions are either crowded out or brought into the listening process.

   If it is appropriate, covenant together to practice the spiritual discipline of silence in preparation for your next meeting.

   a. Talk together with your guide about your experiences of silence.

   b. Record what happens when you practice silence.

Review and Closing

1. Reflect together about your work with the practices of a holy life, the means of grace, and spiritual discernment.

2. What questions or insights do you want to share?

3. Assess where you stand in your journey and your sense of God's call to Christian vocation at this point in the process.

4. Review the notes for the next session and decide what to prepare in advance.

5. Create a closing moment using some of the suggested resources.

Resources

Needed during session

Bible
The Book of Discipline of the United Methodist Church
The United Methodist Book of Worship
The United Methodist Hymnal

Recommended books

Edwards, Tilden. *Living Simply Through the Day*. New York: Paulist Press, 1977.

May, Gerald. *The Awakened Heart: Living Beyond Addiction*. San Francisco: HarperCollins Publishers, 1991.

Morris, Danny. *Yearning to Know God's Will: A Workbook for Discerning God's Guidance in Your Life*. Grand Rapids, Mich.: Zondervan Publishing House, 1991).

Shawchuck, Norman, and Job, Rueben P. *A Guide to Prayer*. Nashville: Upper Room Books, 1988.

Thompson, Marjorie J. *Soul Feast: An Invitation to the Christian Spiritual Life*. Louisville, Ky.: The Westminster Press/John Knox Press, 1995.

Williams, Colin W. *John Wesley's Theology Today*. Nashville: Abingdon Press, 1972.

Hymns and prayers

From *The United Methodist Hymnal*
"Prevenient Grace," #337-360
  "Repentance, "#351-360
"Justifying Grace," #361-381
  "Assurance," #368-381
"Sanctifying and Perfecting Grace," #382-536
  "Personal Holiness (Acts of Piety)," #395-424
  "Social Holiness (Acts of Mercy)," #425-449
"The Power of the Holy Spirit, In Praise of the Holy Spirit," #328-336
"Prayer of John Chrysostom," #412

"Come, Divine Interpreter," #594
"Canticle of Covenant Faithfulness," #125
"An Invitation to the Holy Spirit," #335

From *The United Methodist Book of Worship*
"Teach Me to Hear in Silence," #194

Session 4

Your Heritage And Influences: Common And Unique

*I am reminded of your sincere faith, a faith that lived first in your grandmother
Lois and your mother Eunice and now, I am sure, lives in you.*

(2 Timothy 1:5)

Centering Moments

God's Promise Realized through Faith

For the promise that he would inherit the world did not come to Abraham or to his descendants through the law but through the righteousness of faith. If it is the adherents of the law who are to be the heirs, faith is null and the promise is void. For the law brings wrath; but where there is no law, neither is there violation.

For this reason it depends on faith, in order that the promise may rest on grace and be guaranteed to all his descendants, not only to the adherents of the law but also to those who share the faith of Abraham (for he is the father of all of us, as it is written, "I have made you the father of many nations.")

Romans 4:13-17

Notes:

Purpose of this session::

In this session the seeker is invited to reflect on his or her identity as shaped by family heritage, education, work, and wider community influences on her or his life. This reflection may provide clues to God's leading in the seeker's life in order to discern God's calling now.

Introduction

As guide, be prepared to discuss the meaning of identity, if necessary, and how persons come to a growing awareness of the influences that have shaped self-understanding.

Through this process, you are invited to take intentional steps in your spiritual journey. A first step is to confess, or acknowledge, who you really are in relation to God and the world around you, so you can then share God's love through what you say and do.

One way to begin a discussion of identity is to quickly list responses to the phrase "I am. . . ." (e.g., daughter, husband, teacher, creative, honest, loved by God).

For this session, let the Holy Spirit lead you to form your response to what God is saying to you through the influences on your life: family heritage, education, volunteer and paid work, local church, and experiences in the wider community. Reflecting on these influences and the way they have shaped your identity may help you discern God's direction for your future Christian service.

Influences on your identity and discernment of God's calling come through four major clusters of relationships. The influences of these relationships are unique to each person and help shape your personal and vocational identity. Influences common to all United Methodists that also affect your identity and discernment of God's calling can be explored in "Session 7."

1. Influence of Family Heritage
- your family of origin
- your current family relationships

2. Influences of Education, Volunteer and Paid Work
- educational experience
- volunteer experience
- paid work experience

3. Local and Wider Church Influences

4. Influences of the Wider Community
- community experiences
- world experiences

Organize this exploration of the influences in your life to fit your own experiences. You may arrange your study of these clusters of relationships in the way that seems most useful to you.

Notes:

Discuss the meaning and relationship of heritage and influences and their impact on personal and vocational identity.

A heritage is something that is passed on to you such as culture, property, values, traditions, resources, priorities, and procedures.

An influence is something or someone who affects your understanding of who you are and your discernment of God's calling.

A heritage may also influence you, just as other influences become part of your heritage.

Notes:

Prior to this session, have the seeker consider experiences in his or her family, work, local church, and community.

Find at least one reminder (photograph, document, award, story, etc.) from each of these settings to bring for discussion at this session.

As the guide, you may also bring reminders of your own journey.

Influence of Family Heritage

Your Family of Origin

You are like everyone else. You were born of a human mother and father, and set among caregivers in a particular family structure. You learned a native language and you have been affected by the many changes that the twentieth century has brought to the world. In many, many ways you are connected to and influenced by others.

Like everyone else, God calls you to make sense out of your life, to seek the highest good, to decide whether to do good or harm, to respond to God's message as expressed in the Gospels, and to love God, others, and yourself.

1. What characteristics, traits, skills, and/or interests have you inherited from your family of origin?

2. In what ways are you like your parents? siblings? How are you different?

3. How have your family experiences prepared you for service in the world?

UNDERSTANDING GOD'S CALL: A MINISTRY INQUIRY PROCESS   67

You are unique. No one else, even an identical twin, is exactly like you in every detail. You have your own identity. Even if you and your siblings grew up in the same home, you each had slightly different families when seen from the standpoint of each family member.

1. What was your family structure during your childhood and adolescence? Picture your significant relationships at ages 1, 6, 11, and 16 years using circles, colors, stick figures, or some other symbol to represent you and each member of your family.

2. What influence did family relationships have on your spiritual growth? How do these relationships affect your identity and your discernment of God's calling now?

Notes:

As guide, be prepared to give an example of your response to this question: How would you describe your family from your place in it? Then put yourself in the place of another family member and describe your family (for example as daughter, middle child, grandparent).

An alternate approach to #1 would be to bring various colors of construction paper cut into geometric shapes. A name and a relationship indicator (Alice, mother; Tom, brother) could be written on each piece, then the pieces arranged in relationship to each other.

Talk about how family relationships shape personal and vocational identity.

With roots and wings. You are deeply rooted in your family of origin, whatever its composition. Across your early years, primary caregivers (mother, father, siblings, other relatives, step-parents, and others) provided nurture for your development. They shaped you as a person with roots for stability and wings to fly as an independent person.

1. Identify the major caregivers in your earlier life and describe at least one gift that each person has given to you.

2. What major disruptions such as deaths, divorces, disasters, change of residence occurred in your childhood and adolescence?

3. How do these caregivers and disruptions affect your identity and your discernment of God's calling now?

Your Current Family Relationships

As an adult, you have taken control of your life and assumed the responsibilities and privileges of being a citizen of this world. As an adult, you have created your own household and your new family situation.

1. Diagram or describe your current family household and relationships. If you are single you may want to describe relationships with your primary community.

Notes:

Making vocational decisions is not an individual act done in isolation. There may be repercussions for family and friends, such as the possibility of uprooting families to new locations, or family members who are not supportive of a ministry vocation, or distance from supportive community.

Together imagine how different vocational possibilities might affect family relationships and friendships, as well as other sources of supportive community.

2. Describe at least one positive and one negative experience, past and/or present, with your family or primary community.

3. How might your career decisions affect those closest to you?

4. How do these close relationships affect your identity and your discernment of God's calling now?

Influence of Education, Volunteer and Paid Work

Notes:

Education and work are very important in most Protestant traditions, including the United Methodist tradition.

Education passes on the human heritage to new generations so they can learn about God's world through languages, history, natural and social sciences, arts, and other areas of study. Education also prepares people to use their talents in God's service.

Work is the way you participate in God's creative activity in the world. In your church's heritage, both paid and volunteer work are seen as the stewardship of talents and resources, a way of expressing love for God and others.

Your work in the world may be parenting, being a responsible student, or serving meals to the homeless. Or your service may be given in the "world of work" that includes the specifics of a job, a vocation (trade or profession), and a career path consisting of a series of jobs in a given field of work.

As guide, be prepared to talk about your understanding of the impact of education, volunteer, and paid work experiences.

What is the relationship between work and service?

Education Experience

Experiences you have had in education influence how you discern God's calling to you.

1. Describe your education experiences.

2. What characteristics or skills have you developed out of your own experiences in education?

3. How have your education experiences prepared you for further service in the world?

4. How have or how do your education experiences affect your identity and your discernment of God's calling now?

Volunteer Work Experience

Work you have done as a volunteer influences how you discern God's calling to you.

1. Describe your volunteer work experiences.

2. What characteristics or skills have you developed out of your own experiences in volunteer work?

3. How have your volunteer experiences prepared you for further service in the world?

4. In what ways do your volunteer work experiences affect your identity and your discernment of God's calling now?

Paid Work Experience

Experiences you have had in paid work influence how you discern God's calling to you.

1. Describe your paid work experiences.

2. What are some work skills you now have? Which skills do you like to use? Which skills give you a sense of confidence?

3. Which tasks or jobs do you dislike?

4. In what ways do your paid work experiences affect your identity and your discernment of God's calling now?

UNDERSTANDING GOD'S CALL: A MINISTRY INQUIRY PROCESS   75

Reflection

Reflect on this session so far and be open to the Holy Spirit's leading. How do your heritage and life influences affect your discernment of God's calling now?

In what ways is God leading you either to continue in your current work or to change to a different job or career?

1. How does your current work fulfill your call to service in the world?

2. If you are considering a change in your career direction, which skills can you continue to use in the new career, and which will not be needed?

3. If you choose to continue in your current education or work situation, what changes in your attitude or perspective on your work would you like to make?

Local and Wider Church Influences

Your participation in the various ministries of a local church also influences your identity and discernment of God's calling.

1. Describe your local and/or wider church experiences (such as youth group, district training events, annual conference meetings).

2. What characteristics or skills have you developed out of your church experience?

3. Name pastors and/or other church leaders who have been especially helpful or hurtful to you. How?

4. What church experiences do you especially value or treasure?

5. What church experiences have been most hurtful or disappointing to you?

6. How have your church experiences affected your identity and your discernment of God's calling now?

Influences of the Wider Community and World

This section points to the influences from clusters of relationships in your neighborhood, the sports and hobby groups in which you are, or have been, involved, your ethnic or racial identity and relationships, your gender, your political involvements, and the associates and friendships you have had through networks. The natural world and environmental concerns are also influences on you.

Wider Community

1. Describe your experiences in the wider community (such as encounters with persons or groups from backgrounds different from your own, experiences in community service, sports teams, or involvement in social issues such as environmental concerns).

2. What characteristics and skills have you developed out of your own experiences in the wider community?

3. How have your experiences in the wider community prepared you for further service in the world?

4. How have your experiences in the wider community affected your identity and your discernment of God's calling to you?

World Experiences

1. Describe any global experiences you have had (such as Volunteers in Mission, foreign exchange student program, or travel for recreation or study).

2. What characteristics and skills have you developed out of your global experiences?

3. How have your global experiences prepared you for further service in the world?

4. How have your experiences in the world affected your identity and your discernment of God's calling to you?

Review and Closing

Reflect on insights from this session with your guide.

1. How do you now relate your own influences, experiences, talents, and resources to your discernment of God's calling, guidance, and nurture for your future?

2. Think about the heritage you have received from your family that you cannot change such as race or gender. How do (have) these characteristics affect your relationships in education, work, church, wider community, and world?

3. Which issues, questions, or concerns do you want to explore in more depth?

4. Review the notes for the next session and decide what to prepare in advance.

5. Close your session by naming gifts you have received from your family heritage and the influences in your life. Use the resource list on page 82 to help you create an appropriate ending for this session.

Resources

Needed during session

The United Methodist Book of Worship
The United Methodist Hymnal

Recommended books

Banks, Robert, ed. *Faith Goes to Work: Reflections from the Marketplace.* Bethesda, Md.: The Alban Institute Inc., 1993.

Crabtree, Davida Foy. *The Empowering Church: How One Congregation Supports Lay People's Ministries in the World.* Bethesda, Md.: The Alban Institute Inc.,1989.

Hawkins, Thomas R. *Claiming God's Promises: A Guide to Discovering Your Spiritual Gifts.* Nashville: Abingdon Press, 1992.

McGinnis, James. *Journey into Compassion: A Spirituality for the Long Haul.* New York: Orbis Books, 1993.

Menking, Stanley J. and Barbara Wendland. *God's Partners: Lay Christians at Work.* Valley Forge, Pa.: Judson Press, 1993.

Meyers, Eleanor S., ed. *Envisioning the New City: A Reader on Urban Ministry.* Louisville, Ky.: The Westminister Press/John Knox Press, 1992.

Diehl, William. *The Monday Connection: A Spirituality of Competence, Affirmation and Support in the Workplace.* San Francisco: HarperCollins Publishers, 1991.

Wilke, Richard B. *Signs and Wonders: The Mighty Work of God in the Church.* Nashville: Abingdon Press, 1989.

Hymns and Prayers

From *The United Methodist Hymnal*
See the following categories in the Index of Topics and Categories, page 934.
"Heritage"
"Home and Family"
"Work, Daily"
"Church"

From *The United Methodist Book of Worship*
"Labor Day," #443
"At The Beginning Of A New Job," #538
"For Disciples In The Marketplace," #539
"For Those Who Work," #540
"For Those Who Are Unemployed," #541
" For Those In Military Service," #542

Session 5

Hearing God's Call To Your Future

For surely I know the plans I have for you, says the Lord, plans for your welfare and not for harm, to give you a future with hope.

(Jeremiah 29:11)

Centering Moments

For thus says the Lord: . . .For surely I know the plans I have for you, says the Lord, plans for your welfare and not for harm, to give you a future with hope. Then when you call upon me and come and pray to me, I will hear you. When you search for me, you will find me; if you seek me with all your heart, I will let you find me, says the Lord, and I will restore your fortunes and gather you from all the nations and all the places where I have driven you, says the Lord, and I will bring you back to the place from which I sent you into exile.

Jeremiah 29:10-14

Notes:

Purpose of this session:

In this session, the seeker is invited to consider in more depth two major facets of her or his spiritual journey:

1. *the seeker's own process for listening and responding to God through spiritual discernment in relation to his or her work in the world*

2. *the seeker's current vocational callings and decisions (education and career goals, experiences, and plans)*

Introduction

Before meeting together, read this session and add notes concerning each of the major topics. Review the notes on your heritage from "Session 4."

Come to the session with your notes and descriptions of how you become aware of (or sense) God's calling in your life.

Participating in this process is part of discerning the direction of your continuing spiritual journey.

Spiritual discernment is listening to God and being open to the Holy Spirit's leading. Through the Holy Spirit, God calls you, heals you, nurtures and teaches you, and sends you out to serve.

In discernment, your listening to God may involve consulting with others and comparing your experiences and perspectives to test the genuineness of God's calling in both current and new directions for ministry.

1. How do you listen to God? Who helps you hear God's direction for you?

UNDERSTANDING GOD'S CALL: A MINISTRY INQUIRY PROCESS   89

2. Discernment involves clarifying the goals and images of the future toward which God is leading you. What biblical models, characters, or stories help you focus your search?

3. What pictures and thoughts emerge in your response to the question, "What does God want me to do with my life?"

4. How do you visualize yourself in 10 to 20 years? What do you hope to be doing? In what setting do you see yourself?

Notes:

Listening and Responding to God

With your guide, explore your own process for listening and responding to God in relation to your work in the world. This is your spiritual discernment process.

Three Facets of Spiritual Formation

Talk about what the phrases spiritual formation, Christian identity, and Christian vocation mean to you.

Spiritual formation is an intentional process of opening one's self to God so that he or she may be transformed by God's love into a more Christ-like person.

Spiritual formation includes developing Christian identity and vocation in the Christian community. It has to do with the way you are formed or shaped as a Christian for a life of discipleship.

Read Matthew 22:36-40 and root references in Deuteronomy 6:5, Leviticus 19:18, and others you find.

Spiritual formation has at least three major components that correspond to the Great Commandment to love God, others, and self.

How would you picture or diagram these three components of spiritual formation? Use shapes cut from construction paper to indicate possible relationships.

Reaching **toward** God through prayer, Scripture study, contemplation, worship, and participation in the Christian community.

Reaching **inward** to the depth of your own being through meditation, solitude, and reflection.

Reaching **outward** to others and all creation through active service.

Although these three discrete dimensions are used to describe spiritual discernment and formation, in real life these categories of relationships overlap. Each dimension involves the other two, like a finely cut gem that, when rotated, reflects light from each facet in a different way yet is still one gem.

You may sense God through private meditation and active service as well as through community worship. You become more aware of yourself not only through reaching inward to your most private thoughts and images but also in your experiences of worship and service.

As you reach out to others in service, you may also become more aware of God and more aware of yourself in those relationships with others.

1. When are you most aware of God?

2. When are you most aware of your own spiritual needs and possibilities?

3. When are you most aware of the needs of others and how do you respond?

Becoming More Aware of Discernment Aspects

Spiritual formation is opening yourself to God for transformation. As you grow in your ability to be open to God, discernment is seeing where God is active in the world and in your own life. Discernment is paying attention to God's guidance and direction.

In your discernment process there are at least three powerful influences on you: images, language, and behaviors. With the help of the Holy Spirit and your guide you can transform these into aids to your spiritual discernment.

Images and memories. An image intended to be positive may be distorted because of associations you add to it. For example, parent-child images of God as Father or Mother may elicit negatives for you if your experiences as a child or parent have been hurtful and damaging. At the other extreme, your image of a parent may be so idealistic as to be unrealistic, deny shortcomings, or limit your own individuality and choices.

1. List some images of God that are helpful to you in discerning God's calling to you now.

2. Some images of God may not be helpful to you. Which images of God cause you difficulty in your relationship with God? How are you working with these images?

UNDERSTANDING GOD'S CALL: A MINISTRY INQUIRY PROCESS

Words and language. Language is your code system that helps you communicate ideas, feelings, meanings, values, and other aspects of life. Your language may limit your awareness of God's callings which then affects your responses. Language sets persons apart as well as brings them together. Within a language, every person also has several vocabularies, each related to some dimension of life, such as family, work, or leisure.

Knowing a second language may allow you to become more aware of how your native language has shaped you. You may even appear to be a different person or display a different facet (or face) of yourself according to which language or culture you are using.

1. In what ways does your language influence how you sense and discern God's calling?

2. What words, phrases, metaphors, or other aspects of your language help you to talk about God's calling?

3. How do you cope with times when language limits how you communicate your awareness of God?

Behaviors. Principles and values are communicated through actions and words, and through stories about what people do. As noted in "Session 4," your own culture may blind or distort your awareness of God's calling through the lives of others. Culture is the accumulation of behaviors and stories into preferred patterns.

1. Which actions, such as quiet retreat, service to others, and/or community worship, help you to hear, sense, or pay attention to God?

2. Which stories or reports of dedication, love, and service have increased your sense of God's calling to you?

Reflection

Reflect on this session so far and be open to the Holy Spirit's leading. What have you learned about your spiritual discernment process? How do you become aware of God's guidance and direction?

Connecting Your Calling and Heritage

Notes:

As guide, your role is to facilitate the discussion process so that the seeker makes connections between life's influences and the work of the Holy Spirit.

Some questions to discuss:
- *How is/was God at work in these relationships?*

- *How is God using these relationships to confirm your call?*

- *If these relationships are not supportive of your sense of call, in what other ways do you experience God's guidance?*

In "Session 4: Your Heritage and Influences—Common and Unique," you identified major influences in your life now. Review these influences as they relate to God's calling to you.

1. Recall the ways your relatives help or hinder you in hearing God's call (*see pages 66-70, in this guidebook*).

2. In response to God's call you may make changes in your own career goals. How would possible changes affect your current family or primary community relationships (spouse, children, others closest to you)?

3. Which associates in education and work (such as colleagues, managers, employers, teachers, advisors) encourage you in responding to God's call (pages 71-75)?

UNDERSTANDING GOD'S CALL: A MINISTRY INQUIRY PROCESS   97

4. Which church experiences (local parish, district, annual conference, etc.) invite you to re-examine God's calling to you now (pages 76-77)?

5. What relationships do you see between God's call to be part of Christ's body, the church, and God's call to work in the world?

6. Consider persons you know who are outside your family, work, and church. Which persons have encouraged you to see God's calling in new ways (pages 78-80)?

7. Which community, national, world, and/or environmental experiences have impacted you and been a channel for God to call you?

Calling and Vocation

Both profession and vocation come out of religious meanings. A profession is the act of taking vows of a religious community or accepting a calling requiring specialized knowledge and often long and intensive preparation. The root meaning of vocation is a call from God to serve the common good, to make vocal and express one's calling.

1. At this point in the process, how do you define your work and career in relation to God's call?

2. How is your current career or educational stage and situation related to God's call to you to continue or change in some way?

UNDERSTANDING GOD'S CALL: A MINISTRY INQUIRY PROCESS   99

3. How is God using the opportunities and challenges of work positions that are available to you to call you to faithful service?

4. If you need to be paid, who will pay you for the service you give to the needs of the world? If you serve without pay, who wants or needs your ministry as a volunteer?

5. How is the Holy Spirit now working through your life relationships to enable you to discern your own callings, needs, abilities, and next assignments?

Review and Closing

As you describe your sense of God's calling in your life now, explore how all of the many factors converge for you. With your guide discuss these factors and seek to identify God's call to you:

1. How do you discern (discover, hear, see, sense, figure out) the leading of the Holy Spirit as you fit together your interests, talents, preparation, skills, abilities, and personality?

2. Talk with your guide about how your experience meets four criteria for recognizing God's call:

   - It is something God wants done.
   - It matches and challenges your particular gifts.
   - It is work that you find meaningful.
   - Others in the Christian community affirm you in doing this.

3. Review the notes for the next session and decide what to do in advance.

4. Close with a sharing time using resources from the list on page 105 as appropriate. Many additional hymns and prayers about discerning God's call are in *The United Methodist Hymnal* section on "Called to God's Mission," #568-594.

Resources

Needed during session

Bible
The United Methodist Hymnal

Recommended books

Bolles, Richard N. *Three Boxes of Life and How to Get Out of Them.* Berkeley, Calif.: Ten Speed Press, 1981.

Coffin, William Sloan. *Passion for the Possible: A Message to U.S. Churches.* Louisville, Ky: The Westminster Press/John Knox Press, 1993.

Farnham, Suzanne, et al. *Listening Hearts: Discerning Call in Community.* Harrisburg, Pa.: Morehouse Publishing Co., 1991.

Hopewell, James F. *Congregations: Stories and Structures.* Philadelphia, Pa.: Augsburg Fortress Publishers, 1987.

Lechman, Judith C. *The Spirituality of Gentleness: Growing Toward Christian Wholeness.* San Francisco: Harper & Row, 1987.

Palmer, Parker J. *The Active Life: A Spirituality of Work, Creativity, and Caring.* San Francisco: HarperCollins Publishers, 1992.

Parker, Simon. *The Call to Servant Leadership.* Nashville: Division of Diaconal Ministry, General Board of Higher Education and Ministry, 1990.

Roth, Bob. *Answering God's Call for Your Life.* Nashville: Division of Ordained Ministry, General Board of Higher Education and Ministry, The United Methodist Church, 2006.

Rubey, Sharon G., editor. *The Christian As Minister.* Nashville: General Board of Higher Education and Ministry, 2009.

Yoder, John. *The Politics of Jesus: Vicit Agnus Noster.* Grand Rapids, Mich.: Wm. B. Eerdmans Publishing Co., 1972.

Hymns and Prayers

From *The United Methodist Hymnal*
See the following categories in the Index of Topics and Categories, page 934.
"Called to God's Mission," #568-594
"Discipleship and Service" #201-338
"Call to the Christian Life," #337-349.
From *The United Methodist Book of Worship*
"For Blessing, Mercy, And Courage," #500
"For Discernment," #510
"For Guidance," #512
"For Wisdom," #525

Session 6

Living Your Spiritual Heritage

Therefore, since we are surrounded by so great a cloud of witnesses, let us also lay aside every weight and the sin that clings so closely, and let us run with perseverance the race that is set before us, looking to Jesus the pioneer and perfecter of our faith, who for the sake of the joy that was set before him endured the cross, disregarding its shame, and has taken his seat at the right hand of the throne of God.

(Hebrews 12:1-2)

Centering Moments

"How Can We Name a Love"

*How can we name a love
that wakens heart and mind,
indwelling all we know
    or think or do
    or seek or find?
Within our daily world,
in every human face,
    Love's echoes sound
    and God is found,
hid in the commonplace.*

*If we awoke to life
upheld by loving care
that asked no great reward
    but firm, assured,
    was simply there,
we can, with parents' names,
describe, and thus adore,
    love unconfined,
    our Father kind,
our Mother strong and sure.*

*So in a hundred names,
each day we all can meet
a presence, sensed and shown
    at work, at home,
    or in the street.
Yet names and titles all,
shine in a brighter sun:
    In Christ alone
    is love full grown
and life and hope begun.*

Notes:

An alternate way to focus your time together is to share the act of "Daily Prayer and Praise" from The United Methodist Book of Worship, (569-578). Then read or sing the hymn, "How Can We Name A Love?" (The United Methodist Hymnal, #111) and describe who God is and how God relates to you using the words of the hymn.

The United Methodist Hymnal, **#111**
Words: Brian Wren, 1975
Wren uses these words to assure us that we can see God's presence in the world in many ways.
Words © 1975, 1995 by Hope Publishing Co., Carol Stream, IL 60188. All rights reserved. Reprinted under CCLI No. 1766914.

Notes:

Purpose of this session:

This session is designed for seekers and guides to increase their awareness of how spiritual perspectives give form and meaning to call and are a part of the discerning of God's direction and of decisionmaking.

Your Spiritual Inheritance

To prepare for this session, read "Doctrine and Discipline in the Christian Life" ¶101, section 1, and "Theological Guidelines: Sources and Criteria" in the Discipline, ¶104, section 4.

It is a common human longing that people want to make sense of their lives. People interpret what happens out of various perspectives. Faith is one perspective through which experience is interpreted. Seeing the world through the eyes of faith gives meaning to your life and experience in light of your relationship with God.

As you proceed with the *Ministry Inquiry Process,* your reflection will be influenced by what you have learned through your life experience and by your faith.

This guidebook provides some ways for you to name your values, standards, and beliefs, as a way to help you get in touch with how God is at work in your life.

1. Your decisions are based on what you value. Some values have been instilled in you by your family of origin, some through public education, some as a result of life experiences, and some from your church.

   a. Think about a time in your life when you had to make an important decision.

   b. Name some values you used in making the decision, and where you learned them, such as "My mother/father always taught me to. . . ."

UNDERSTANDING GOD'S CALL: A MINISTRY INQUIRY PROCESS 107

2. Read or sing together the first verse of "I Want Jesus to Walk with Me" (*The United Methodist Hymnal*, #521).

    a. Talk with your guide about what it means to have Jesus walking with you on your life journey.

    b. How does the image of Jesus walking with you affect the way you look at life and your decision making?

Understanding Faith

In order to talk about how your spiritual perspective or faith affects your life and calling, you need to have some understanding of what faith is.

1. Talk with your guide about what the word "faith" means to you.

    How would you explain faith to someone who had never heard the word before?

Notes:

As guide, help the seeker find other words that the hymn writers use as symbols of faith and be prepared to share your ideas about the relationship between faith and the terms listed here.

2. Look at hymns dealing with the subject of faith (listed on page 941 in *The United Methodist Hymnal*) and see what understandings of faith you can find represented.

3. How is faith related to other words or images the hymn writers use to represent faith such as:

   a.   belief

   b.   obedience

   c.   trust

   d.   hope

   e.   confidence

   f.   other _____

UNDERSTANDING GOD'S CALL: A MINISTRY INQUIRY PROCESS 109

The Way of Salvation

Notes:

The *Book of Discipline* contains this statement, "Faith is the only response essential for salvation" (¶101). What do you think faith means in this statement?

John Wesley struggled throughout his life with a question of faith, *"What must I do to be saved?"* In his early life, he focused on what he felt **he had to do** for salvation and diligently followed a variety of spiritual practices in an attempt to be obedient to God's will.

Later, Wesley received assurance that he was saved by God's grace. He came to understand salvation as **God's act** of grace on humanity's behalf through Jesus Christ AND the **response** of faithful Christians in loving God, loving neighbor, and all creation.

Faith and good works are forever linked in Wesleyan theology. Spiritual practices such as studying the Scripture and praying lead to works of service for others as a way of loving God in response to God's love for humanity and all creation.

In the Wesleyan tradition, **the way of salvation** is a process of

- *recognizing one's sinfulness and repenting of all sin,*
- *receiving God's love and assurance that sins are forgiven, and*
- *growing more Christlike in daily living*

through the perfecting love of the Holy Spirit.

1. Talk with your guide about your understanding of salvation. What is salvation? What does God do? What are you to do? What is the role of faith in salvation?

As guide, be prepared to discuss the relationship of faith and salvation.

2. The Wesleyan tradition teaches that persons will experience three kinds of grace in their spiritual journeys: *prevenient*, *justifying*, and *sanctifying*. *The United Methodist Hymnal* organizes hymns around the three kinds of grace and provides a glimpse of a Wesleyan understanding of the way of salvation.

Prevenient grace means that God's love and forgiveness is already available to each person through the presence and work of the Holy Spirit. The Holy Spirit works in the lives of all. This prevenient grace helps persons become aware of their own sinfulness and of their need for forgiveness.

a. With your guide, look at the section on prevenient grace, *The United Methodist Hymnal*, #337-360. Note here words or phrases that explain prevenient grace and how persons are to respond to God's persistent love.

- prevenient grace

- response to God's persistent love

When persons repent of their sin and receive assurance or knowledge that God has forgiven them, they have experienced God's act of **justifying** grace. This grace is the result of God's love for humanity expressed through the life, death, and resurrection of Jesus Christ. A person who has this experience of forgiveness is transformed for a new life. Sometimes this is called conversion or new birth.

b. Now examine the section on justifying grace, *The United Methodist Hymnal*, #361-381. Note here words or phrases that explain justifying grace. Also describe how persons are to respond to God's redemptive love.

- justifying grace

- response to God's redemptive love

Sanctifying grace is God's ongoing work in those who have been justified. Even persons who have experienced justification or conversion continue to grow. The Holy Spirit's perfecting love works in these Christians so they grow more Christlike in their daily living.

c. Now look at the section on sanctifying and perfecting grace, *The United Methodist Hymnal*, #382-536. Note here words or phrases that explain sanctifying and perfecting grace and how persons can respond to God's nurturing love.

- sanctifying and perfecting grace

- response to God's nurturing love

UNDERSTANDING GOD'S CALL: A MINISTRY INQUIRY PROCESS 113

3. Reflect on these three kinds of grace. What do they mean to you? Where have you seen God's grace at work in your own life and relationships?

4. How would you tell someone about prevenient, justifying, and sanctifying grace in your own words? Which distinctions and contrasts are helpful?

Reflection

Reflect on this session so far and be open to the Holy Spirit's leading. What have you learned about faith and the way of salvation?

Living Your Faith
Through Discipleship

John Wesley taught the early Methodists that Christian faith should be evident in the way they lived. To say it another way, Christian belief should be reflected in a Christian lifestyle. The "General Rules of the Methodist Church" provided a guiding discipline for those first Methodists who wanted to lead Christian lives.

1. Review these general rules in ¶103 in the *Book of Discipline*.

2. Talk with your guide about these rules, then state what the following mean in your own words, giving examples when appropriate.

    a. The first rule is: Do no harm, by avoiding evil of every kind.

    b. The second rule is: Do good of every possible sort, and, as far as possible, to all.

UNDERSTANDING GOD'S CALL: A MINISTRY INQUIRY PROCESS   115

c. The third rule is: Attend upon all the ordinances of God.

3. Compare your examples with those Wesley gave to the Methodist societies.

Reflection

Reflect on this session so far and be open to the Holy Spirit's leading. What have you learned about your spiritual inheritance—values, faith, belief, discipleship?

Through the Eyes of Faith

Theological Guidelines

The Wesleyan heritage provides resources and standards for interpreting your life experience and making decisions through the eyes of faith.

1. With your guide, read and discuss Section 4 on "Theological Guidelines: Sources and Criteria" in *The Book of Discipline* (¶104).

2. Reflect on your participation in this process using the four theological guidelines (sometimes called the Wesleyan quadrilateral):

1. Scripture

a. Think of a person in Scripture like yourself who faced a similar discernment about Christian vocation. Find a Scripture passage that relates to your listening to God's call.

b. What can you learn from Scripture that guides your decision making in this process?

2. *Tradition*

a. Think about the tradition of the church. What has the church taught over the centuries about what it means to be Christian and what it means to answer God's call?

b. What examples do you know of persons in history responding to God in their lives?

c. What standards of behavior have been passed on to you through your church?

3. Experience

    a.   How did your life experience affect your decision about participating in the *Ministry Inquiry Process*?

    b.   Have you ever experienced God's presence or the working of the Spirit in your life?

    c.   Can you see God at work in this time of reflection and discernment? How?

4. Reason

a. Talk with your guide about how reason is at work in this process.

b. How do reason and discernment fit together?

c. Why do you suppose God gave us the ability to reason?

Social Principles

In addition to theological guidelines, The United Methodist Church provides other guidelines for decision making:

"The Social Principles (¶¶160-166) provide our most recent official summary of stated convictions that seek to apply the Christian vision of righteousness to social, economic, and political issues. Our historic opposition to evils such as smuggling, inhumane prison conditions, slavery, drunkenness, and child labor was founded upon a vivid sense of God's wrath against human injustice and wastage." (*Book of Discipline*, ¶101)

1. With your guide, select a portion of the Social Principles to read and discuss together. How is the shared faith of United Methodists evident in these principles?

2. Select one social issue to discuss and answer the questions:

   a. How does your faith help you understand and respond to this social issue?

   b. What kinds of ministries are needed in response to this issue?

Review and Closing

1. Share questions and/or learnings from today's session.

2. Review notes for next session and decide what to prepare in advance.

3. Create a closing worship moment to reflect your time together by selecting a hymn and a prayer from the resource list, or share a prayer of thanksgiving that God's presence is with you through the Holy Spirit in times of discernment and decision making (*The United Methodist Book of Worship*, #556, #557).

Resources

Needed during session

The Book of Discipline of the United Methodist Church
The United Methodist Book of Worship
The United Methodist Hymnal

Recommended books

Rubey, Sharon G., editor. *The Christian As Minister*. Nashville: General Board of Higher Education and Ministry, The United Methodist Church, 2009.

Williams, Colin W. *John Wesley's Theology Today*. Nashville: Abingdon Press, 1972.

Wuellner, Flora Slosson. *Prayer, Fear, and Our Powers: Finding Our Healing, Release, and Growth in Christ*. Nashville: Abingdon Press, 1989.

Hymns and prayers

From *The United Methodist Hymnal*
"We've a Story to Tell to the Nations," #569
"I Want Jesus to Walk with Me," #521
"God of the Sparrow, God of the Whale," #122
"How Can We Name a Love," #111
"Canticle of Wisdom," #112
"Hope of the World," #178
"Woman in the Night," #274
"Where He Leads Me," #338
"Lord, Speak to Me," #463
"For Guidance," #366
"Prayer for a New Heart," #392
"For Courage to do Justice," #456
"The Prayer of Saint Francis," #481
"Three Things We Pray," #493

From *The United Methodist Book of Worship*
"For Guidance," #512
"For the Mind of Christ," #514
"A Prayer of Saint Patrick," #529
"General Prayers of Thanksgiving," #556
"General Prayers of Thanksgiving," #557

Session 7

Your United Methodist Heritage

"There is one body and one Spirit, just as you were called to the one hope of your calling, one Lord, one faith, one baptism . . . ."

(Ephesians 4:4-5)

Centering Moments

God ever faithful,
In a time of great need you raised up your servant John Wesley
To preach the good news of redemption and the life of holiness:
Revive your work among us
That inspired by the same faith
And upheld by the same grace in Word and Sacrament,
We may love you and our neighbor faithfully in our own time,
Through Jesus Christ, our Lord. Amen.

**The Character of a Methodist: A Service of Worship in Readings and Song"
Copyright © 2002 The United Methodist General Board of Discipleship, PO Box
340003, Nashville TN 37203-0003; telephone: (615) 340-7073; Worship Web
site: www.umcworship.org. All rights reserved. Used by permission.**

Notes:

The listing of Book of Discipline *references to the church at the beginning of this session provides an overview of the many ways that United Methodist theology, church structure, and ministries are interrelated.*

Specific sections from the Book of Discipline *may be selected to examine in more depth. These sections should be read in advance of this session with notes taken for discussion in your time together.*

Purpose of this session:

This session is an opportunity for a seeker to explore her or his United Methodist heritage in more depth.

Introduction

In this session, you have an opportunity to examine in more detail the heritage that members of The United Methodist Church share. This shared heritage is defined and described in the "Historical Statement" and "Parts I, II, IV" of the *Book of Discipline*:

"Historical Statement"

Part I: "The Constitution" describes the current denominational structure and organization.

Part II: "Doctrinal Standards and Our Theological Task"
"Section 1—Our Doctrinal Heritage"
"Section 2—Our Doctrinal History"
"Section 3—Our Doctrinal Standards and General Rules"
"Section 4—Our Theological Task"

Part IV: "Social Principles"

Scan each of these sections and then note those that are especially important for you. You may already have read some of these references as part of previous studies. Bring your notes, comments, and questions to the session.

Uniting Faith and Good Works

Early leaders in the Methodist, United Brethren, and Evangelical Association such as John and Charles Wesley, Philip Otterbein, Martin Boehm, Thomas Coke, Francis Asbury, and others emphasized the connection between faith and good works (see *Book of Discipline*, Part II, ¶101).

We see God's grace and human activity working together in the relationship of faith and good works. Gods' grace calls forth human response and discipline" (Book of Discipline, ¶101).

UNDERSTANDING GOD'S CALL: A MINISTRY INQUIRY PROCESS   129

This emphasis on God's grace and human response has been a major part of our tradition ever since.

1. Talk with your guide about what it means to unite faith and good works.

2. United Methodists share a common heritage with other Protestant traditions. Examine the shared beliefs in "Basic Christian Affirmations," *Book of Discipline*, Part II, ¶101. Which of these are familiar to you? Are there any that raise questions for you?

3. United Methodist heritage is also unique. Which of the distinctive Wesleyan emphases, *Book of Discipline*, ¶101, do you most value?

The Theological Task

United Methodists are expected to think about their *faith* in order to make decisions about *acting* on God's behalf in meeting needs in the world. When you reflect about your relationship with God and God's work in the world, you are thinking theologically.

> *Theology is our effort to reflect upon God's gracious action in our lives. In response to the love of Christ, we desire to be drawn into a deeper relationship with the "author and perfecter of our faith." Our theological explorations seek to give expression to the mysterious reality of God's presence, peace, and power in the world. By so doing, we attempt to articulate more clearly our understanding of the divine-human encounter and are thereby more fully prepared to participate in God's work in the world.*
>
> (Book of Discipline, ¶104)

1. Talk with your guide about how and when you have reflected on "the divine-human encounter" and "God's work in the world." What do you still want to learn about theological reflection?

UNDERSTANDING GOD'S CALL: A MINISTRY INQUIRY PROCESS   131

2. A more complete description of the theological task of United Methodists is found in ¶104 in the *Book of Discipline*. How is your own faith expressed in these principles?

3. Sometimes called the "Wesleyan quadrilateral," Scripture, tradition, experience, and reason are essential guidelines for the theological task of The United Methodist Church and its ministries (*Book of Discipline*, ¶104). How do Scripture, tradition, experience, and reason help you with your own spiritual discernment?

Reflection

Reflect on this session so far and be open to the Holy Spirit's leading. What have you learned about your United Methodist tradition?

Notes:

Review your notes on the "General Rules" in "Session 6, Living Your Spiritual Heritage," pages 114-115 in this guidebook.

Continue the discussion here if needed or go on to the next section.

The General Rules

The General Rules were written for early Methodists who wanted to organize Methodist societies. A society was similar to your congregation in that it met regularly for teaching and worship. Each member of a society was also a member of a class that met weekly to support that person's growth in faith and good works.

Three general rules are found in ¶103 in the *Discipline*. These rules were intended to provide some guidance about how faithful Christians could respond in love to God's grace through good works.

1. Summarize these three rules and memorize your summary. For example, *"Do no harm, do all the good you can, participate in all the means of grace that God gives us."* Then review the examples given for each rule.

2. How can/do you apply the General Rules as guidelines in your own life?

3. Which examples of each rule are especially significant for you in your own spiritual journey today?

Notes:

Review your notes on the Social Principles in "Session 6" on page 120 in this guidebook in preparation for your discussion.

Social Principles

The Social Principles of The United Methodist Church are similar to the "General Rules" in that they provide guidance for how the church is to respond in love to God's grace through good works in today's world (*Book of Discipline*, Part IV).

> *The Social Principles are a prayerful and thoughtful effort on the part of the General Conference to speak to the human issues in the contemporary world from a sound biblical and theological foundation as historically demonstrated in United Methodist traditions. They are intended to be instructive and persuasive in the best of the prophetic spirit. The Social Principles are a call to all members of The United Methodist Church to a prayerful, studied dialogue of faith and practice (Book of Discipline, Part IV).*

The General Conference of The United Methodist Church meets every four years with representatives from each annual conference to deal with matters of faith and good works. The Social Principles are reviewed and updated at each General Conference in order to provide guidance for United Methodists in the practice of faith through good works.

1. Talk with your guide about the meaning of the statement from the "Social Principles" printed above. How does this statement relate to your own spiritual discernment?

UNDERSTANDING GOD'S CALL: A MINISTRY INQUIRY PROCESS

2. Review highlights of the Social Principles in Part IV of the *Discipline*. In what specific ways are the three influences (family, work, community) considered in Session 4 also addressed in the United Methodist social principles? Some examples:

Family and marriage

Work and career

Community and world

3. With which principles do you disagree or feel uncomfortable?

4. Which principles do you view as being especially significant or valuable for you?

Notes:

Various perspectives on baptism were also discussed on pages 29 and 144 in this guidebook. Review your notes and compare responses in your discussion here.

Baptism and the Lord's Supper

Baptism

Baptism points to your own decisions to commit your life to Christ and live as a Christian. Through renewal of your baptismal vows, you can assume full responsibility for commitments that parents or others made on your behalf when you were an infant or child.

1. Consider the statements about baptism contained in the *Discipline*, ¶103, Article XVII. Talk with your guide about what these statements mean to you.

   In baptism the congregation is called to nurture you and support you in your spiritual discernment of your calling, work, and ministry as a baptized Christian.

2. Examine in detail the services for Christian baptism found in *The United Methodist Hymnal*, 32-54. Where do you find instances of congregational nurture and support?

UNDERSTANDING GOD'S CALL: A MINISTRY INQUIRY PROCESS 137

3. Baptism identifies a person by a new name, "Christian" or "disciple." How did acquiring the name Christian affect your life?

4. Your parents (or other caregivers) shaped your identity in many ways. If you were baptized as an infant, at which points in your life have you consciously committed yourself to God?

Lord's Supper

The Lord's Supper is a reminder of the meals Christ shared with all persons, of Christ's giving his body and blood. It is a remembrance and participation in the life, death, and resurrection of Jesus Christ. This sacrament renews your relationship with God and is a time of thanksgiving and celebration.

1. Consider the statements about the Lord's Supper contained in the *Discipline*, ¶103, Article XVIII. How is the Lord's Supper defined and described in these statements?

2. Examine in detail the services for the Lord's Supper found in *The United Methodist Hymnal*, 6-31. Where do you find instances of remembering, of being connected with God and with others?

3. How have you experienced "communion" with others?

4. How do these experiences form the basis for your current spiritual journey?

Review and Closing

Talk with your guide about your United Methodist heritage:

1. What parts of this tradition have shaped your life?

2. What new discoveries have you made?

3. What questions remain for you about your United Methodist heritage? How will you answer them?

4. In what ways does your understanding and experience of United Methodist history, doctrine, and mission influence your discernment? your calling?

5. Review the notes for the next session and decide what to prepare in advance.

6. With your guide, create a closing for this session using the suggested resources or resources of your own choosing.

Resources

Needed during session

The United Methodist Book of Discipline
The United Methodist Hymnal

Recommended books

Jones, Paul W. *Theological Worlds: Understanding the Alternative Rhythms of Christian Belief*. Nashville: Abingdon Press, 1989.

Madsen, Norman P. *This We Believe*. Nashville: Graded Press, 1987.

Hymns and prayers

From *The United Methodist Hymnal*
See the following categories in the Index of Topics and Categories, page 934.
"Baptism"
"Faith"
"Grace"
"Heritage"
"Holy Communion"
"Justice"
"Mission and Outreach"
"Social Concerns"
"Work, Daily"

Session 8

What Gift Can I Bring?

Now there are varieties of gifts, but the same Spirit; and there are varieties of services, but the same Lord; . . .

(1 Corinthians 12:4-5)

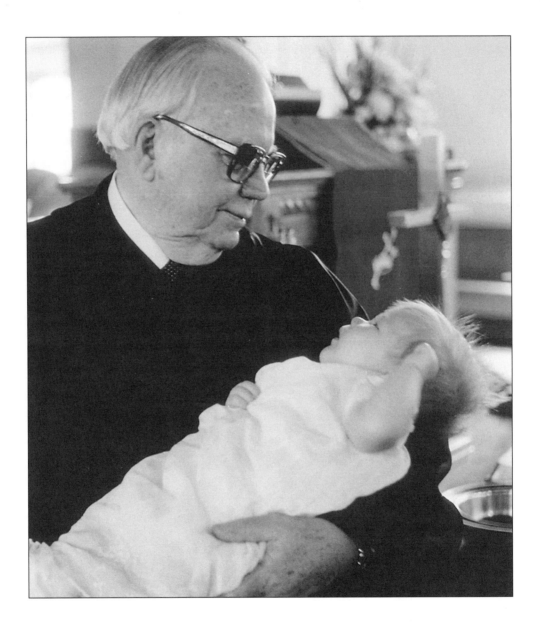

UNDERSTANDING GOD'S CALL: A MINISTRY INQUIRY PROCESS   143

Centering Moments

"What Gift Can We Bring"

What gift can we bring, what present, what token?
What words can convey it, the joy of this day?
When grateful we come, remembering, rejoicing,
what song can we offer in honor and praise?

Give thanks for the past, for those who had vision,
who planted and watered so dreams could come true.
Give thanks for the now, for study, for worship,
for mission that bids us turn prayer into deed.

Give thanks for tomorrow, full of surprises,
for knowing whatever tomorrow may bring,
the Word is our promise always, forever;
we rest in God's keeping and live in God's love.

The United Methodist Hymnal, **#87, verses 1-3**
Words: Jane Marshall, 1980
In this hymn, Marshall expresses thanks for the gifts of life and asks what gifts we can bring to God's world.
Words © 1982 by Hope Publishing Co., Carol Stream, IL 60188. All rights reserved.
Reprinted under CCLI No. 1766914.

Notes:

Purpose of this session:

The purpose of this session is to provide an opportunity for the seeker to consider in more depth any factors or issues that might affect her or his decision about continuing in the ministry of the laity or moving into candidacy for ordained ministry.

What Gift Can I Bring?

Baptism and the Ministry of All Christians

In preparation for this session, read the baptismal service and vows in The United Methodist Hymnal, *33-39.*

Ministry involves discipleship and service, as well as helping others to be faithful Christians in love of God and love of neighbor. What does the ministry of all Christians require?

1. Explore some of the hymns and prayers listed under "Discipleship and Service" in *The United Methodist Hymnal*, 940.

    Write some phrases about what is expected of those who are part of the ministry of all Christians.

UNDERSTANDING GOD'S CALL: A MINISTRY INQUIRY PROCESS   145

2. United Methodists believe persons are initiated into the church at
   baptism.

   a. Talk with your guide about what it means to be "initiated into Christ's
      holy church."

Notes:

Review your notes about baptism as calling on pages 29 and 136-137 in preparation for this discussion.

   b. Record phrases that indicate what is expected of baptized Christians.

3. Think of a lay person who is a good role model for faithful discipleship.
   How does that person's life reflect what it means to be part of the ministry
   of all Christians?

Notes:

As guide, be prepared to guide this discussion by giving appropriate examples from your own growth in faith.

Another way to reflect on gifts is to have the seeker list adjectives that others might use to describe him or her.

As guide, be prepared to offer various adjectives as possibilities.

Your Inheritance

Growing into a faithful Christian requires a process of learning and growing as God works through new experiences and new relationships in your life.

You do not have to know everything about your faith. What is important is that you are willing to learn through your experiences and to claim responsibility for your own behavior.

Some things about yourself that you bring to ministry cannot be changed such as your age, gender, ethnicity, childhood experience, cultural background, special talents or abilities, and native language. These factors all affect your discernment and decision making about a vocation in ministry.

Reflect on the gifts your inheritance has provided for your faith journey.

- What do you like to do?

- What can you do well?

- What makes your heart sing?

- What awards or honors have you received?

- How do others describe you?

Use the chart on the next page to record your answers to questions 1-3:

1. "What gift can we bring, what present, what token?" (*The United Methodist Hymnal*, #87) What talents or abilities do you bring to ministry?

2. "Give thanks for the past, for those who had vision, who planted and watered so dreams could come true." (*The United Methodist Hymnal*, #87) Name those persons in your life who have been important in growing your dream of ministry.

3. "Give thanks for tomorrow, full of surprises." (*The United Methodist Hymnal*, #87)

    a. What strengths does your inheritance give you for the surprises of ministry?

    b. What do you still want to learn about yourself or others?

    c. What do you want to share with others?

UNDERSTANDING GOD'S CALL: A MINISTRY INQUIRY PROCESS 147

What Have I Inherited?

Talents and abilities	**Example:** a gift of music		
Important persons	**Example:** a teacher		
Still to learn	**Example:** how I can best use my gift of music in ministry		

Reflection

Reflect on this session so far and be open to the Holy Spirit's leading. What have you learned about baptism and discipleship and the gifts you can bring?

Strategies for Growth and Change

As a living human being and growing Christian, you are always in a process of becoming. God continues to work in your life through the Holy Spirit for growth and renewal.

1. As you think about how to live out your faith through Christian vocation, assess your strengths and discuss vocational options with your guide.

a. Review the book *Answering God's Call for Your Life* to see if any special interests emerge for you.

- Note some possible church vocations—chaplain, youth worker, pastor, missionary, curriculum writer—that seem to fit you. How might you live out your faith through these vocations?

- Note some other vocations that seem to fit you, such as pilot, social worker, teacher, nutritionist, nurse. How might you live out your faith through these vocations?

b. On the chart below, select two or three vocational options that interest you. Then list the talents and skills needed for this vocation. Evaluate which talents and skills you bring.

Vocation	Talents and skills required	Talents I bring

UNDERSTANDING GOD'S CALL: A MINISTRY INQUIRY PROCESS   151

2. What have you learned about your talents and abilities for ministry?

    a. What areas of growth and change are needed?

    b. What do you need to know more about?

    c. What skills do you need to develop more fully?

    d. What questions or unresolved issues do you still have?

3. Examine your list of areas for growth and decide which items have the highest priority.

a. What are the most important areas for growth that you want to pursue?

b. With your guide, plan a strategy for pursuing these areas of growth such as trade or business school, college, graduate school. Interview others about ways to prepare for a specific career.

Review and Closing

1. As a seeker, share what have you learned about yourself and your vocation in ministry.

2. As a guide, share observations or assessments you have about gifts the seeker brings to ministry and areas of needed growth.

3. Review strategies and next steps. Note any advance preparation for the next session you will do together.

4. Review the notes for the next session and decide what to prepare in advance.

5. Read or sing "How Like A Gentle Spirit," *The United Methodist Hymnal*, #115, and select a prayer from the resource list for a closing thanksgiving that you have an opportunity to serve God through ministry.

Resources

Needed during session

Roth, Bob. *Answering God's Call for Your Life*. Nashville: Division of Ordained Ministry, General Board of Higher Education and Ministry, 2006.

The United Methodist Hymnal

Recommended books

Johnson, Reginald. *Your Personality and the Spiritual Life*. Wheaton, Il.: Victor Books, 1988.

Parker, Simon. *The Call to Servant Ministry*. Nashville: Division of Diaconal Ministry, General Board of Higher Education and Ministry, The United Methodist Church, 1990.

Rubey, Sharon G., editor. *Christian As Minister*. Nashville: General Board of Higher Education and Ministry, The United Methodist Church, 2009.

Hymns and Prayers

From *The United Methodist Hymnal*
"What Gift Can We Bring," #87
"There's a Wideness in God's Mercy," #121
"Holy Spirit, Come Confirm Us," #331
"Where He Leads Me," #338
"Take Time to Be Holy," #395
"O Jesus, I Have Promised," #396
"I Am Thine, O Lord," #419
"The Voice of God Is Calling," #436
"Forth in Thy Name, O Lord," #438
"Lord, Speak to Me," #463
"Faith, While Trees Are Still in Blossom," #508
"Whom Shall I Send?" #582
"Here I Am, Lord," #593

"Baptism of the Lord," #253
"Prayer to the Holy Spirit," #329
"Prayer for a New Heart," #392
"For True Life," #403
"For Courage to Do Justice," #456

Session 9

Ministry Options
to Explore

I have called you by name, you are mine.

(Isaiah 43:1b)

Centering Moments

"When the Poor Ones"

When the poor ones who have nothing share with strangers,
when the thirsty water give unto us all,
when the crippled in their weakness strengthen others,
then we know that God still goes that road with us.

When at last all those who suffer find their comfort,
when they hope though even hope seems hopelessness,
when we love though hate at times seems all around us,
then we know that God still goes that road with us.

When our joy fills up our cup to overflowing,
when our lips can speak no words other than true,
when we know that love for simple things is better,
then we know that God still goes that road with us.

The United Methodist Hymnal, **#434, verses 1-3.**
Words by J.A. Olivar and Miguel Manzano; trans. by George Lockwood.
Based on Matthew 25:31-46. This hymn reminds us that God often uses those who are in great need to minister to us.
© 1971, J. A. Olivar, Miguel Monzano and San Pablo International—SSP. All rights reserved. Sole U.S. Agent: OCP Publications, 5536 NE Hassalo, Portland, OR 97213. Reprinted under CCLI No. 1766914.

Notes:

Prior to this session, explore ministry options by reading from the Book of Discipline
- *¶¶125-131*
  ¶¶137-138, 315.2; 328-329, 332-334, 343-344

The seeker should interview three persons representing each of the ministry options discussed in this session. See ideas for questions on the pages in this guidebook indicated below. Bring notes from interviews for discussion in this session.

- *page 161, "Servant Ministry"*
- *page 165, " Ministry of the Deacon in Full Connection"*
- *page 166, "Ministry of the Elder"*

Purpose of this session:

The purpose of this session is to give the seeker an opportunity to explore specific ministry options and come to some clarity about her or his response to God's call.

Introduction

In this closing session of the *Ministry Inquiry Process*, you will have an opportunity to explore specific ministry options and to decide what the next steps in your spiritual journey will be.

The United Methodist Church has supported you through your guide on this part of your spiritual journey. Now you will work with your guide to discern the direction for your ministry in the world.

Ministry Options

Notes:

Servant Ministry

All Christians are called to ministry in the world. In a sense, you have an opportunity to become God's hands and feet and heart in the world through your ministry.

> The heart of Christian ministry is Christ's ministry of outreaching love. Christian ministry is the expression of the mind and mission of Christ by a community of Christians that demonstrates a common life of gratitude and devotion, witness and service, celebration and discipleship. All Christians are called to this ministry of servanthood in the world to the glory of God and for human fulfillment. . . . (Book of Discipline, ¶125).

Read Part III, "The Ministry of All Christians," Sections I-III, ¶¶120-133 (*Book of Discipline*).

Talk with your guide about what the ministry of all Christians means to you.

As guide, be prepared to share your understanding of the ministry of all Christians and ministry of the laity.

Begin to think about ministry as stewardship of resources for God's work in the world.

Find a way such as a diagram, poster, or collage to depict the relationship between the different forms of ministry indicating the gifts each brings to doing the work of God.

Read Section IV in "The Mission and Ministry of All Christians" (*Book of Discipline*, ¶¶134-136) and discuss them with your guide.

1. What does servant ministry mean to you?

2. Can you identify any of the stages of spiritual growth and transition in your own life?

3. Are the ministry of all Christians, ministry of the laity, and Christian discipleship the same? Related? How would you define each of these terms?

4. Interview a person you know who is a good role model of the ministry of all Christians. Ask questions such as: How has your relationship with God developed over your lifetime? How does being Christian affect your daily life? How are you in ministry in the world? What are the gifts of discipleship? What are the challenges?

5. If you were to continue as part of the ministry of the laity in response to God's call, how would your servant ministry be expressed through your vocation?

UNDERSTANDING GOD'S CALL: A MINISTRY INQUIRY PROCESS   163

Servant Leadership

Read Section V in "The Ministry of All Christians" (*Book of Discipline*, ¶¶137-138).

Within The United Methodist Church, there are those called to servant leadership, lay and ordained. Such callings are evidenced by special gifts, evidence of God's grace, and promise of usefulness. (Book of Discipline, ¶137)

1. Talk with your guide about what servant leadership means.

2. Share your ideas about the meaning of this sentence: *Ordained ministers are called by God to a lifetime of servant leadership in specialized ministries among the people of God.* (¶138)

Clergy Orders

Read Section II in "The Ministry of the Ordained" (*Book of Discipline*, ¶¶305-309).

1. With your guide, discuss the meaning of "Orders in Relation to the Ministry of all Christians," ¶305.

2. Review the purposes for an Order in ¶307. What are the advantages in belonging to an Order? Disadvantages?

UNDERSTANDING GOD'S CALL: A MINISTRY INQUIRY PROCESS   165

The Ministry of a Deacon in Full Connection

Notes:

Read ¶¶138, 328-331 in the *Book of Discipline* about the church's understanding of "The Ministry of a Deacon."

As guide, prepare yourself for this discussion by reviewing ¶¶138, 328-331 about the ministry of a deacon in full connection.

1. Talk with your guide about the understanding of the ministry of a deacon in these paragraphs.

2. Interview a deacon in full connection about his or her understanding of ministry. Ask questions such as: Why do you believe the ministry of a deacon in full connection is a faithful response to God's call? What kind of ministry do you have? What are the benefits of this ministry? What are the challenges? What special qualities or skills are needed for this kind of ministry?

Add the ministry of a deacon to your depiction of stewardship of resources for God's work in the world.

How is the ministry of a deacon in full connection related to the ministry of all Christians?

What does the ministry of a deacon bring to God's work in the world?

3. If you were to enter the ministry of a deacon in response to God's call, how would your ministry be expressed through your vocation?

Notes:

As guide, prepare yourself for this discussion by reviewing ¶¶138, 332-344 about the ministry of an elder.

Add the ministry of an elder to your depiction of stewardship of resources for God's work in the world.

How is ordained ministry related to the ministry of all Christians?

What does the ministry of an elder bring to God's work in the world?

The Ministry of Elder

Read ¶¶138, 332-344 in the *Book of Discipline* about the church's understanding of "The Ministry of an Elder."

1. Talk with your guide about the understanding of the ministry of an elder in these paragraphs.

2. Interview an elder about her or his understanding of ministry. Ask questions such as: Why do you believe the ministry of an elder is your most faithful response to God's call? What kind of ministry do you have? What are the benefits of the ministry of an elder? What are the challenges? What special qualities or skills are needed for this kind of ministry?

3. If you were to enter the ministry of an elder in response to God's call, how would your ministry be expressed through your vocation?

Listening Into Your Own Future

Notes:

As you now seek to be aware of God's call to you, select one or more of the following to guide your response.

This section begins a process of intentionally narrowing the focus to one form of ministry.

1. *There is but one ministry in Christ, but there are diverse gifts and evidence of God's grace in the Body of Christ (Ephesians 4:4-16). (Book of Discipline, ¶130)* Read ¶130 in the *Book of Discipline* and talk with your guide about what it means to you.

As guide, it is particularly important for you not to impose your hopes and wishes on the seeker.

This is a time of discernment on behalf of the seeker through clarifying questions, sharing feedback, and supporting the seeker's own discernment.

2. Review some of the significant biblical examples of calling, sending, and serving such as Isaiah 6, Mark 3:13-19, Luke 10, Acts 2-6, Romans 12. How do these passages help you discern your response to God's call?

3. Re-examine your vows of baptism and church membership (*The United Methodist Hymnal*, 32-54). How do they assist in your discernment of God's calling now?

4. What part do your own heritage and influences, experiences, talents, and resources play in your discernment of God's calling, guidance, and nurture for your future?

5. Which issues, questions, or concerns do you want to explore in more depth?

Reflection

Reflect on this session so far and be open to the Holy Spirit's leading.

1. Summarize what you have learned about yourself and your gifts for ministry through this process.

2. Have your guide share insights with you about your gifts and how they might fit the different ministry options.

3. To which ministry option (ministry of the laity, ministry of a deacon in full connection, or ministry of an elder) is God calling you? Why do you think so? Explore your choice in more depth now.

Responding to God's Call

Notes:

This section of the Ministry Inquiry Process *involves a deeper study of standards for ministry defined in the* Book of Discipline.

Work with the ministry form selected by the seeker.

Examples of how standards can be drawn from the Book of Discipline *are given for each form of ministry.*

The United Methodist Church expects that persons in ministry will meet or exceed certain standards. As you move toward your response to God's call, this section provides an opportunity to assess how your life fulfills these standards and to identify areas for growth.

Some factors of your life that affect your readiness for ministry may be changed, such as the way you understand yourself and your inheritance, your understanding of family relationships, the way you relate to other persons, and your lifestyle. Reflect on these factors as you move toward a decision about your response to God's call.

Some factors in your life may be fixed, such as your age, ethnic or racial heritage, gender, and natural abilities. Reflect on how these aspects of your identity affect your decision about your response to God's call.

Work through the information about standards and entrance into the ministry option you have identified for yourself at this time.

The Ministry of the Laity

1. The *Book of Discipline* clearly states standards for all members of The United Methodist Church (¶¶125-131) and the vows for membership in The United Methodist Church (*The United Methodist Hymnal*, 34-52). Examine these standards and fill in the columns below.

Standards for Members	Strengths I Bring	Areas for Growth
Example: - Faith in God, Jesus Christ, and the Holy Spirit	- Lifelong faith	- Learn more about the Holy Spirit

2. With your guide talk about how you currently express the ministry of the laity. Map out some ways your faith journey may continue through prayer and other Christian disciplines, Scripture, retreats, workshops, mission experiences, and other educational or renewal events in your local church, district, or annual conference.

3. If you are thinking of changing vocations, review *Answering God's Call for Your Life,* by Bob Roth. A list of possible vocational options can be found in "Session 8, What Gift Can I Bring?"

4. Contact the General Board of Discipleship for more information about lay ministry options is:

   Director Connectional Laity Development
   GBOD
   PO Box 340003 Nashville, TN 37203-0003
   (877) 899-2780, ext. 7179
   szeigler@gbod.org

5. For more information about General Ministry, read *The Monday Connection: A Spirituality of Competence, Affirmation, and Support in the Workplace* by William Diehl that explores five types of ministry in daily life: competency, presence, ethics, change, and values.

UNDERSTANDING GOD'S CALL: A MINISTRY INQUIRY PROCESS   173

The Ministry of the Ordained

1. Read Section I in "The Ministry of the Ordained" (*Book of Discipline*, ¶¶301.1-304) and the vows for ordination in *The United Methodist Book of Worship*, 665-666 and 674-676. Fill in the columns below.

Qualifications for Ordination	Strengths I Bring	Areas for Growth
Example: - Have ". . . gifts for ordained ministry, evidence of God's grace in their lives, and promise of future usefulness in the mission of the Church" (¶304.1g).	- Background in teaching	- How teaching is part of minister's role and responsibility

2. Are there other issues related to your family, marital status, interpersonal relationships, lifestyle, sexuality, physical challenges, and the United Methodist way for both itinerating and non-itinerating appointments that you need to discuss with your guide in relationship to a vocation in ordained ministry?

3. Read Section II in "The Ministry of the Ordained" (*Book of Discipline*, ¶¶310-314), about entrance procedures and candidacy for licensed and ordained ministry. Talk with your guide about what you have learned about what is expected for candidacy in ordained ministry. List your strengths and growing edges as you think about yourself in ordained ministry.

UNDERSTANDING GOD'S CALL: A MINISTRY INQUIRY PROCESS   175

4. Examine the qualifications for election to provisional membership and
    commissioning in ¶324. The general qualifications are listed here. Make
    note of questions and ask your guide for clarification.

    • Candidacy requirement

    • Service requirement

    • Undergraduate requirement

    • Other educational requirements

    • Alternate educational requirements

    • Official transcript

    • Health certificate

    • Written and oral doctrinal examination

    • Recommended by 3/4 vote of district committee on ordained ministry

    • Personal interview

    • Notarized statement regarding felony, misdemeanor, or sexual
       misconduct

    • Autobiographical statement

5. What are some other words or images you might use for commissioning (¶325)?

6. What does it mean to be a provisional member of an annual conference in The United Methodist Church (¶¶326-27)?

7. The steps into candidacy in ordained ministry are outlined in *The Christian As Minister*. With your guide, map out your next steps in order to enter candidacy for ordained ministry.

8. The candidacy registrar for your annual conference Board of Ordained Ministry is:

_____
Name

_____
Address

_____

_____
Telephone

6. For more information about the history of the ministry of the deacon, read *The Deacon: Ministry Through Words of Faith and Acts of Love* by Ben L. Hartley and Paul E. Van Buren.

7. For more information about Ordained Ministry, read *The Yoke of Obedience: The Meaning of Ordination in Methodism* by Dennis M. Campbell, *The Orders of Ministry in The United Methodist Church* by John E. Harnish, *The Orders of Ministry: Problems and Prospects* by Hendrik R. Pieterse and *QR Classics*.

Review and Closing

This is the final session of the *Ministry Inquiry Process*. As you come to the end of this part of your spiritual journey, spend some time with your guide in review.

1. ***Our Mutual Commitment.*** Review your original commitment to see how you have progressed. How well have you achieved each of your goals? What questions still remain?

2. **Further Steps.** Consult with your guide about resources for any additional topics and concerns you want to explore on your own as part of your own discernment process. Decide together which sessions and activities will be most useful for you to do as you create your personalized plan for further exploring.

3. **Outcome Report.** With your guide, write a brief report of your learning and discernment in the *Ministry Inquiry Process*. With your permission, your guide will keep a copy of this report.

Note ideas about what you might share in the report here:

You are responsible for keeping this outcome report for use in a candidacy track if you choose one.

If you continue into candidacy for ordained ministry, you can use your report to summarize your journey thus far and introduce yourself to the next stage.

4. ***Next Steps in Ministry.*** Discernment is not completed when you finish the *Ministry Inquiry Process*. This is just the beginning. Every day is a process of discerning what God wants you to do with your life.

If you are continuing in the ministry of the laity, outline the steps you will take for your own growth and renewal. See "Appendix C" on page 198 for denominational resources for ongoing spiritual growth.

If you are continuing toward candidacy for ministry as a deacon in full connection or ministry as an elder,

  a. your guide should send a letter to the candidacy registrar of the conference Board of Ordained Ministry certifying that you have completed the *Ministry Inquiry Process*, if your annual conference requires it, and

  b. you should send a letter to the candidacy registrar for the conference Board of Ordained Ministry and indicate your interest in candidacy. Include the information that you have completed the *Ministry Inquiry Process* and that your guide will send a letter certifying that completion.

5. ***Closing.*** With your guide, a) read and discuss Luke 4:18-19, b) share how you will continue to discern God's call and celebrate the gifts you have shared with each other in this process, c) close with "When the Poor Ones" (*The United Methodist Hymnal*, #434) and a prayer.

Resources

Needed during session

Bible
The Book of Discipline of the United Methodist Church
The United Methodist Book of Worship
The Christian As Minister
The United Methodist Hymnal

Recommended books

Campbell, Dennis M. *The Yoke of Obedience: The Meaning of Ordination in Methodism*. Nashville: Abingdon, 1988.

Roth, Bob. *Answering God's Call for Your Life*. Nashville: Division of Ordained Ministry, General Board of Higher Education and Ministry, 2006.

Hymns and prayers

From *The United Methodist Hymnal*:
See the following categories in the Index of Topics and Categories, page 934
"Call to the Christian Life"
"Commitment"
"Discipleship and Service"
"Installation Services"
"Jesus Christ, Example"
"Ordination"
"Mission and Outreach"
"Testimony and Witness"
"Work, Daily"

From *The United Methodist Book of Worship*:
"A Litany for the Church and for the World," 495
"General Prayers of Thanksgiving," 556
"Dismissal, Blessings, and Closing Prayer," 559
"A Celebration of New Beginnings in Faith," 588
"An Order for Commitment to Christian Service," 591

Annotated Bibliography

This bibliography is an annotated list of suggested resources for the *Ministry Inquiry Process* by session. The essential United Methodist resources are necessary for the entire process. In addition, it would be helpful to have two or three versions of the Bible available for comparison and discussion.

Essential United Methodist Resources

Each session of the *Ministry Inquiry Process* relies on basic United Methodist resources:

The Book of Discipline of the United Methodist Church. The *Discipline* provides the heritage and understanding of The United Methodist Church through foundational historical and theological statements, a plan for self-governance, and a statement of social principles which guide lives of discipleship.

The United Methodist Book of Worship © 1992. This book is the basic resource for worship in the United Methodist Church and reflects Anglican, Evangelical United Brethren, and Methodist heritage. Liturgies for worship and prayers for many occasions are included in this important resource.

The United Methodist Hymnal © 1989. From the beginning, Methodists have been known as "a singing people." This resource not only includes hymns from diverse ethnic sources, but also creeds, prayers, and services for Sunday worship, celebration of the sacraments, and other times of worship.

Session 1: Sharing Your Faith Story

González, Justo. *Mentors as Instruments of God's Call*. Nashville: Division of Diaconal Ministry, General Board of Higher Education and Ministry, 1992 (updated 2003). Biblical reflections help the reader learn of persons who served as instruments of God's call.

Matthaei, Sondra H. *Faith Matters: Faith Mentoring in the Faith Community*. Philadelphia: Trinity Press International, 1996. Discusses the nature and practice of faith-mentoring, as well as preparation for faith-mentoring.

Millard, Kent. *Get Acquainted with Your Christian Faith*, Leader's Guide and Study Book. Nashville: Abingdon, 1996. A workbook addressing how God creates, empowers, and calls us.

Morris, Danny E. *Yearning to Know God's Will: A Workbook for Discerning God's Guidance for Your Life*. Grand Rapids, Mich.: Zondervan Publishing House, 1991. A how-to book on discernment for individuals and groups.

Session 2: The Bible and God's Call

Miller, Wendy. *Learning to Listen: A Guide for Spiritual Friends*. Nashville: Upper Room Books, 1993. This book deals with the listening process especially as it relates to listening to God.

Parker, Simon. *The Call to Servant Leadership*. Nashville: Division of Diaconal Ministry, General Board of Higher Education and Ministry, 1990. Biblical reflections on call and what it means to be a servant leader through meditation, biblical reflection and interaction are explored.

Roth, Bob. *Answering God's Call for Your Life*. Nashville: Division of Ordained Ministry, General Board of Higher Education and Ministry, 2006. This book looks at Christian calls and vocations both in the church and beyond the church.

Session 3: Practicing God's Presence

Edwards, Tilden. *Living Simply Through the Day*. New York: Paulist Press, 1977. Practices for a simple way to be open to the Holy One in daily life.

Job, Rueben and Norman Shawchuck. *A Guide to Prayer*. Nashville: Upper Room Books, 1988. Includes weekly devotional themes and monthly retreat models.

May, Gerald. *The Awakened Heart: Living Beyond Addiction*. San Francisco: HarperCollins Publishers, 1991. Discusses how the invitation of love calls forth and develops the interior life.

Morris, Danny E. *Yearning to Know God's Will: A Workbook for Discerning God's Guidance for Your Life*. Grand Rapids, Mich.: Zondervan Publishing House, 1991. A how-to book on discernment for individuals and groups.

Thompson, Marjorie J. *Soul Feast: An Invitation to the Christian Spiritual Life*. Louisville: The Westminster Press/John Knox Press, 1995. Offers spiritual practices and rule of life as a way to create space where God can nurture us.

Williams, Colin W. *John Wesley's Theology Today*. Nashville: Abingdon Press, 1972. Examines the primary beliefs of John Wesley in comparison to views of the other reformers.

Session 4: Your Heritage and Influences

Banks, Robert, ed. *Faith Goes to Work: Reflections from the Marketplace*. Bethesda, Md.: The Alban Institute Inc., 1991. Testimonies from persons who have discovered the connection between their faith and their work.

Diehl, William. *The Monday Connection: A Spirituality of Competence, Affirmation and Support in the Workplace*. San Francisco: HarperCollins Publishers, 1992. Explores five types of ministry in daily life: competency, presence, ethics, change, and values.

Hawkins, Thomas R. *Claiming God's Promises: A Guide to Discovering Your Spiritual Gifts*. Nashville: Abingdon Press, 1992. This book is about knowing what gifts from God one has and about using them.

McGinnis, James. *Journey into Compassion: A Spirituality for the Long Haul*. New York: Orbis Books, 1993. Explores lives of figures of compassionate commitment plus the practical steps of prayer and fasting for peacemaking and reconciliation.

Menking, Stanley J., and Barbara Wendland. *God's Partners: Lay Christians at Work*. Valley Forge, Penn.: Judson Press, 1993. This book addresses how God is calling lay persons in the places where they live to do God's work in the world.

Willimon, William W. *What's Right with the Church*. San Francisco: Harper & Row, 1985. Explores the incarnational life of the church through stories and experiences of the church.

Session 5: Hearing God's Call to Your Future

Campbell, Dennis M. *Who Will Go for Us? An Invitation to Ordained Ministry.* Nashville: Abingdon Press, 1994.

Coffin, William Sloan. *A Passion for the Possible: A Message to U.S. Churches.* Louisville, Ky: The Westminster Press/John Knox Press, 1993. Discusses love as source of renewal and offers vision for the future that addresses social problems.

Farnham, Suzanne, et al. *Listening Hearts: Discerning Call in Community.* Harrisburg, Penn.: Morehouse Publishing Co., 1991. A manual for discernment groups who can help folks sort out vocational decisions by being active listeners and asking the right questions.

Hopewell, James F. *Congregations: Stories and Structures.* Philadelphia: Augusburg Fortress Publishers, 1987. Stories of congregations and methods for analyzing and understanding them.

Lawson, David J. *Hungering for the Future.* Nashville: Abingdon Press, 1996.

Palmer, Parker J. *The Active Life: A Spirituality of Work, Creativity, and Caring.* San Francisco: HarperCollins Publishers, 1990. Addresses spirituality and spiritual practices for people who live a busy life.

Parker, Simon. *The Call to Servant Leadership.* Nashville: Division of Diaconal Ministry, General Board of Higher Education and Ministry, 1990. Biblical reflections on call and what it means to be a servant leader through meditation, biblical reflection, and interaction are explored.

Rubey, Sharon G., editor. *The Christian As Minister.* Nashville: General Board of Higher Education and Ministry, 2009. Explores vocational options of lay, commissioned, and ordained ministries in response to God's call.

Svennungsen, Ann M., and Melissa Wiginton, eds., *Awakened to A Calling: Reflections on the Vocation of Ministry.* Nashville: Abingdon Press, 2005.

Yoder, John. *The Politics of Jesus: Vicit Agnus Noster.* Grand Rapids, Mich.: Wm B. Eerdmans Publishing Co., 1994. Addresses teachings and ministry of Jesus as a guide to Christian behavior.

Session 6: Living Your Spiritual Heritage

Rubey, Sharon G., editor. *The Christian As Minister*. Nashville: General Board of Higher Education and Ministry, 1997. Explores vocational options of lay, commissioned, and ordained ministries in response to God's call.

Smith, James Bryan. *A Spiritual Formation Workbook: Small Group Resources for Nurturing Christian Growth*. San Francisco: HarperCollins Publishers, 1993. Explores contemplative, holiness, charismatic, social justice, and evangelical traditions for spiritual growth.

Williams, Colin W. *John Wesley's Theology Today*. Nashville: Abingdon Press, 1972. Examines the primary beliefs of John Wesley in comparison to views of the other reformers.

Wuellner, Flora Slosson. *Prayer, Fear, and Our Powers: Finding Our Healing, Release, and Growth in Christ*. Nashville: Abingdon Press, 1989. Many helpful exercises for dealing with fears and opening one's self more to God's power.

Session 7: Your United Methodist Heritage

Carder, Kenneth L. *Living Our Beliefs: The United Methodist Way*. Nashville: Discipleship Resources, 1996.

Felton, Gayle. *By Water and the Spirit: Making Connections for Identity and Ministry*. Nashville: Discipleship Resources, 1997. Leader's guide and participant workbook for study of baptism.

Jones, Paul W. *Theological Worlds: Understanding the Alternative Rhythms of Christian Belief*. Nashville: Abingdon Press, 1989. An examination of five different theological perspectives on faith.

Madsen, Norman P. *This We Believe*. Nashville: Graded Press, 1987. A study guide for the "Articles of Religion and the Confession of Faith" of The United Methodist Church.

Session 8: What Gift Can I Bring?

Mather, Herbert. *Gifts Discovery Workshop*. Nashville: Discipleship Resources, 1985. Presents a group workshop format for a gifts discovery process.

Parker, Simon. *The Call to Servant Leadership*. Nashville: Division of Diaconal Ministry, General Board of Higher Education and Ministry, 1990. Biblical reflections on call and what it means to be a servant leader through meditation, biblical reflection, and interaction are explored.

Roth, Bob. *Answering God's Call for Your Life*. Nashville: Division of Ordained Ministry, General Board of Higher Education and Ministry, 2006. This book looks at Christian calls and church vocations both in the church and beyond the church.

Rubey, Sharon G., editor. *The Christian As Minister*. Nashville: General Board of Higher Education and Ministry, 1997. Explores vocational options of lay, commissioned, and ordained ministries in response to God's call.

Session 9: Ministry Options to Explore

Campbell, Dennis M. *The Yoke of Obedience: The Meaning of Ordination in Methodism*. Nashville: Abingdon, 1988. Examines the development of ministry and the meaning of ordination in the Wesleyan tradition.

Crain, Margaret Ann, and Jack L. Seymour. *A Deacon's Heart: the New United Methodist Diaconate*. Nashville: Abingdon Press, 2001.

Reber, Robert. *Linking Faith and Daily Life: An Educational Program for Lay People*. Bethesda, Md.: The Alban Institute Inc., 1991. An outstanding introductory curriculum designed to help persons connect their faith with their daily life and work.

Roth, Bob. *Answering God's Call for Your Life*. Nashville: Division of Ordained Ministry, General Board of Higher Education and Ministry, 2006. This book looks at Christian calls and church vocations both in the church and beyond the church.

Retreat Resources

Job, Rueben. *A Journey to Solitude and Community*. Nashville: Upper Room Books, 1989. A guided retreat on spiritual formation with participant workbook.

Job, Rueben and Norman Shawchuck. *A Guide to Prayer*. Nashville: Upper Room Books, 1988. Includes weekly devotional themes and monthly retreat models.

Leech, Kenneth. *The Eye of the Storm: Living Spiritually in the Real World*. San Francisco: HarperCollins Publishers, 1992. Living spiritually in the real world . . . an excellent integration of the concern for spirituality and for social justice.

Parker, Simon. *The Call to Servant Leadership*. Nashville: Division of Diaconal Ministry, General Board of Higher Education and Ministry, 1990. Biblical reflections on call and what it means to be a servant leader through meditation, biblical reflection, and interaction are explored.

Smith, James Bryan. *A Spiritual Formation Workbook: Small Group Resources for Nurturing Christian Growth*. San Francisco: HarperCollins Publishers, 1993. Explores contemplative, holiness, charismatic, social justice, and evangelical traditions for spiritual growth.

Appendix A

Models of Spiritual Discernment

Christians through the ages have wanted to do the will of God. Presumably you are one of those persons who is trying to see your gifts and talents as God sees them as well as seeing the needs of the church and mission of Christ in the world. The process of trying to discover what God wants or values is called **discernment**. You are trying to listen to God so as to know God's will.

Another definition of discernment is to see as God sees. In 1 Samuel 16, the great prophet Samuel goes at God's command to anoint a new king of Israel. Samuel knows that the new king is one of Jesse's sons. The sons come before Samuel one by one starting with the oldest. When Samuel sees the oldest son, Eliab, he thinks that surely this son is the one. But God says to Samuel, "Do not look on his appearance or on the height of his stature, because I have rejected him; for the Lord does not see as mortals see; they look on the outward appearance, but the Lord looks on the heart." (1 Samuel 16:7)

What you are really to be about as you move through this guide is learning to see more as God sees especially regarding who you are, what gifts you have been given, the needs of the world, the needs of the mission of Christ in the world and in the church, and how God dreams you can best be a part of God's work in the world.

So discernment is both a state and a process. In discerning the ministry into which you are called on behalf of Christ, there are specific things that you or you and others can do to help you listen to what God wants. That process involves doing things that help you listen to God, sense God's direction, see what God sees.

There are three preconditions to discernment. *The first is to have a relationship to God as we know God through the life, ministry, death, and resurrection of Jesus Christ* as that is manifested in Scripture, tradition, experience, and reason, and as revealed through the activity of the Holy Spirit to and in you. This first precondition means that you know God to be a loving God, who earnestly wants to be in communication with you. As a part of getting to know and to trust God, you discover ways of receiving that communication, of hearing God's voice, of seeing from Christ's perspective, of sensing the loving, healing presence of the Holy Spirit. One of the very important skills needed for discernment is the *ability to receive that communication from God.*

"Session 4" (pages 61-83 in this guidebook) offers a chance for you to reflect on your favorite and best ways to receive God's communication. Any practice you can do to grow in these and/or develop others during the time you are using this study will obviously be helpful to you and to God in your journey of discernment about this question of your ministry on Christ's behalf.

UNDERSTANDING GOD'S CALL: A MINISTRY INQUIRY PROCESS

The second precondition is wanting to know God's will. It is very possible to relate to God without wanting to know what it is that God wants. It is also important to be sure that you are listening to God and not to other voices.

After his baptism, Jesus went into the wilderness to seek God's will. He went off by himself into the desert perhaps thinking he could hear God better there. He wanted to know that what he was hearing was from God. In this story of Jesus' temptations in the wilderness, it is very clear that some of the voices that Jesus heard were not God's voice. But for Jesus it had to be *God's* will.

Christians who practice discernment talk about a concept called "holy indifference." Holy indifference means that we want to know God's will badly enough that we are willing to lay aside any biases or desires that we have so that we may really hear God. Coming to holy indifference may well be the hardest part of the whole process since it means that you have come to the point of wanting God's will more than you want your own.

The third precondition for discernment is committing yourself to doing what you discern God wants. Sometimes there still must be a wrestling inside yourself that must occur, especially if the answer seems not to be the one for which you had been hoping. As an example, it is clear in the temptation story that Jesus became committed to doing what he heard from God, that is, to living his life and doing his ministry the way he discerned that God wanted. But he had to struggle within himself with opposing tendencies; otherwise, the temptations would not have been temptations.

Once you have discerned what you believe to be God's will, you must hold it by faith. You can't be absolutely sure. However, there are some checkpoints that you can use.

- God's will is consistent with the major thrusts of Scripture.
- Often there will be an element of surprise involved.
- Check out what you have come to understand about God's will for you with a spiritually mature Christian whom you trust by asking if in their judgment what you have heard could be the will of God.
- If it is God's will, usually a sense of peace will come, and this sense of peace continues to feel right over time.

Here are six models for discernment that might be helpful to you. The first two are for personal discernment. The others are for discernment by groups.

Models of Personal Discernment

Model 1: Morris Model
This model is taken from *Yearning to Know God's Will* by Danny Morris.

Preconditions

1. A desire to do God's will.
2. An openness to God.
3. An awareness of how God acts in order to recognize God's action.

Process

4. Use conventional methods to choose the best possibility.
5. Ask if this choice is God's will. This question needs to be a "yes" or "no" question, no multiple choice. Then wait patiently for the answer.
6. Consolation (peace, freedom, joy, lightness) or desolation (stifled, not right, uneasiness, anxiety) will come. Over time one of the two will prevail.

Model 2: Gestation

by Susan Ruach

1. Have holy intention of wanting what God wants.
2. Let the question rise up from within your depths, that is be planted in yourself by God. After all, you have to have a question before you can have an answer.
3. Live with the question. Talk about it, rest with it, read with it in mind, work with it.
4. Always be listening.
5. Begin to see form, changing shape to the question. Be aware of kicks, nudges, movement.
6. At some moment you will come to an understanding. It will come to birth in God's own time.

Models for Corporate Discernment

Model 1. Discernment Steps: Toward a Vision of God's Will

by Bishop David J. Lawson

1. One needs good data, basic factual information, identification of alternatives and possibilities.
2. Insist that all categories be kept soft in order that playfulness and creativity may be present and contribute to the process.
3. Maintain holy indifference to the outcome; lay aside all biases, prejudices; be willing to leave the outcome to God's direction and be obedient to the results.
4. Maintain a community and climate of worship.
5. Ask and respond to: Where have you sensed God's benediction in what we have been about?
6. Spend time in reflection, perhaps with a Scripture passage, seeking to listen to God's intimations in the future, hints of God's direction.
7. Share with the faith community what you have heard/seen/felt in your reflection time. Dialogue about what has been reported. Avoid debating for there is no right

UNDERSTANDING GOD'S CALL: A MINISTRY INQUIRY PROCESS 193

or wrong, win or lose, but rather a desire to listen to God. Frequently, insight and wisdom come in the dialogical space with a group.

8. Humility is crucial. Each one must be constantly aware that God may have spoken the definitive word to another person.

9. Sometimes silence is how the Christian community moves ahead.

10. Pause from time to time and ask: "God, are you trying to say anything to us? Are we missing anything here?"

11. Remember holy (sacred) indifference to the outcome. Be willing to receive wisdom or direction even if it does not fit your strong desires or decisions.

12. When agreement is reached, directions, plans, commitments are all offered to God. Sometimes the question: "Are we ready to offer this to God?" is helpful.

Model 2. Fenhagen Model

(from James C. Fenhagen, *Ministry and Solitude*. New York: The Seabury Press, 1981)

Next comes the process of deliberation. When a concern is brought to the surface and agreed upon as important enough to warrant such commitment, all possible evidence is gathered and made available to all who will be engaged in the deliberation. Then the process begins. In brief, it includes the following steps.

1. A period of meditation and prayer seeking openness to and guidance from the Spirit.

2. The sharing of "cons," as each person reports the reasons against moving in a particular direction that he personally discerns.

3. A period of prayer allowing time to reflect on the seriousness of the "cons" that have been shared.

4. A sharing of "pros," as each person reports his own personal discernment. If no consensus emerges, the process continues.

5. A period of prayer allowing time for reflection upon step 4.

6. An effort to sort out and weigh the reasons behind the pros and cons, recording those reasons so that they are available to all, and to discern communally, in the light of what has been listed, the choices to which the community is called by God. In commenting on this aspect of the process, Father Futrell writes, "If the Holy Spirit is working through the second time of election, and if the conditions of authentic communal discernment have been fulfilled (i.e., if there is genuine openness to the Spirit), the decision should be made clear, and confirmation should be experienced unanimously through shared deep peace...finding God together." (John Futrell, S. J. "Communal Discernment: Reflections on Experience," *Studies in the Spirituality of the Jesuits* IV, no. 5 [November 1972]: 173.)

7. A concluding prayer of thanksgiving and the reaffirmation of corporate commitment to carrying out the decision.

At first glance, such a process seems unduly long for the everyday decisions that take place within the life of a parish. That would depend, of course, on the time given to each step.

Appendix B

Group Model

What follows is a group model which could be used in a retreat setting as an optional model for a guide and several seekers in the *Ministry Inquiry Process*.

After the individual introductory session, a retreat or other group model may be used, as long as the importance of time between sessions for reflection and assimilation is recognized. Providing opportunity for individual consultation and guidance will also be crucial if using a retreat model.

Between retreat sessions, seekers may complete assigned tasks such as journaling or interviewing, do advance preparation for the next retreat session, and/or meet individually with a guide. Opportunities for individual time with a guide are crucial for this process.

Please note that this retreat model is not to be a substitute for the seeker's relationship with a guide which is at the heart of the *Ministry Inquiry Process*.

First Session

Friday evening
- Evening meal
- Opening worship
- Introductions
- "Sharing Your Faith Story" (an opportunity for retreat participants to share their spiritual journeys)
- Bible Study (of one biblical call)
- Evening silence until breakfast (time for individual reflection and journaling before bed)

Saturday morning
- Morning prayer
- Breakfast
- "The Bible and God's Call" (more creative exploration of biblical calls)
- Individual reflection time (for being outdoors, journaling, meeting with guide)

Saturday afternoon
- Lunch
- "Your Heritage and Influences" (group works with material from this basic session with time for individual assessment/reflection within the session)
- Break
- Group sharing/reflecting
- Planning ahead (what needs to be done before the next retreat, scheduling individual appointments, etc.

UNDERSTANDING GOD'S CALL: A MINISTRY INQUIRY PROCESS

- Closing worship
- Adjourn

Two or three months may be needed between retreat sessions so that seekers can complete work on the sessions begun here.

Second Session

The second retreat could deal with "Practicing God's Presence" on Friday evening, then "Living Your Spiritual Heritage" and "What Gift Can You Bring?" on Saturday.

Third Session

A third retreat could deal with "Your United Methodist Heritage" and "Ministry Options To Explore" followed by an individual meeting with a guide to do reflection, decision making, and an outcome report. Plan time for celebration through individual and group affirmation.

Appendix C

Denominational Resources for Your Further Growth

The United Methodist Church, as a connectional system, offers many opportunities for ongoing spiritual growth. This is only a beginning list that you may have experienced or wish to attend. As seeker and guide, you may want to name other church activities that were important in your own spiritual journey and helped you identify your place in ministry.

Annual conference sessions - an annual meeting that provides enrichment through worship, study, and work.

Christian Educators Fellowship - an opportunity for persons involved in educational ministry to share on an annual conference, regional, or national level.

Church camps - a place where young and old alike have come to renew their faith and identify their Christian vocation.

Convocations on ministry - a gathering of people who are considering a call to ordained ministry.

Disciple Bible Study - a local church opportunity to learn more about the Bible through long-term, disciplined study.

"Focus" conferences - gatherings of persons involved in educational ministry with children for spiritual enrichment and learning.

General Conference sessions - an opportunity to share in the worship, study, and work of the general church every four years.

Local church Sunday school classes, choir, committees - ways to live out one's faith in faithful service through sharing one's gifts.

Lock-ins - an overnight experience for youth that builds community and provides an opportunity for sharing their faith.

Marriage Enrichment - weekend retreats for couples to renew and enrich their marriage relationship.

Order of Saint Luke - a group devoted to providing ways to grow spiritually.

Spiritual retreats - local, regional, or annual conference opportunities to get away and grow in one's faith.

Teacher training workshops - an opportunity to develop one's gifts for the ministry of teaching.

United Methodist Men - a men's organization for spiritual growth and service.

United Methodist Women - a women's organization that emphasizes mission education and spiritual growth.

United Methodist Youth Fellowship - a local church group emphasizing shared faith and fellowship.

Upper Room Academy for Spiritual Formation - a two-year program of study for spiritual growth.

Volunteers in Mission - opportunities for persons to serve in hands-on service around the world.

Walk to Emmaus - a program of weekend retreats devoted to spiritual renewal.

Youth convocations - national meetings of youth and youth leaders for education, fellowship, and worship.